Stress Management

A WELLNESS APPROACH

Nanette E. Tummers

Human Kinetics

Library of Congress Cataloging-in-Publication Data

Tummers, Nanette.
  Stress management : a wellness approach / Nanette Tummers.
      p. cm.
  Includes bibliographical references and index.
  1. Stress management. 2. College students–Psychology. I. Title.
  RA785.T86 2013
  155.9'042–dc23

                        2012044934

ISBN-10: 1-4504-3166-6 (print)
ISBN-13: 978-1-4504-3166-8 (print)

The web addresses cited in this text were current as of February 19, 2013, unless otherwise noted.

Acquisitions Editor: Cheri Scott; **Developmental Editor:** Ragen E. Sanner; **Assistant Editors:** Anne Rumery and Derek Campbell; **Copyeditor:** Patsy Fortney; **Indexer:** Nancy Ball; **Permissions Manager:** Dalene Reeder; **Graphic Designer:** Nancy Rasmus; **Graphic Artist:** Dawn Sills; **Cover Designer:** Keith Blomberg; **Photograph (cover):** Royalty-Free Imagery/Fotolia; **Photographs (interior):** © Human Kinetics, unless otherwise noted; © Stephen Coburn - Fotolia (p. 1); © Jose Gil - Fotolia (p. 10); © PhotoDisc (pp. 25 and 142); © Alexis Heyraud/Fotolia.com (p. 29); © Pete Saloutos/Fotolia (p. 35); © Monkey Business/Fotolia (pp. 46, 81, 93, and 96); © iStockphoto/Nikada (p. 60); © Blend Images (p. 75); © Getty Images/DAJ (p. 84); © PhotoDisc/Kevin Peterson (p. 87); © Corbis (p. 101); © Andres Rodriguez - Fotolia (pp. 111 and 156); © Brian Weed - Fotolia (p. 114); © Eyewire (p. 122); © MM Productions/Corbis (p. 133); © Greg Hinsdale/Corbis (p. 137); © Yuri Arcurs - Fotolia (p. 146); © Digital Vision (pp. 147 and 163); © pixhunter.com - Fotolia (p. 159); courtesy of Nick Lacy, Eastern Connecticut University (p. 168); **Art Manager:** Kelly Hendren; **Associate Art Manager:** Alan L. Wilborn; **Illustrations:** © Human Kinetics; **Printer:** Edwards Brothers Malloy

Printed in the United States of America   10 9 8 7 6 5

The paper in this book is certified under a sustainable forestry program.

Human Kinetics
Website: www.HumanKinetics.com

United States: Human Kinetics
P.O. Box 5076
Champaign, IL 61825-5076
800-747-4457
e-mail: info@hkusa.com

Canada: Human Kinetics
475 Devonshire Road, Unit 100
Windsor, ON N8Y 2L5
800-465-7301 (in Canada only)
e-mail: info@hkcanada.com

Europe: Human Kinetics
107 Bradford Road
Stanningley
Leeds LS28 6AT, United Kingdom
+44 (0)113 255 5665
e-mail: hk@hkeurope.com

For information about Human Kinetics' coverage in other areas of the world, please visit our website: www.HumanKinetics.com

contents

activity finder

⊛ This icon indicates there is an accompanying worksheet in the appendix. Instructors can download the worksheets from the instructor guide at www.HumanKinetics.com/StressManagement.

> continued

> *continued*

> *continued*

> *continued*

preface

Stress is ubiquitous in our world today. The increase in information and communication as a result of rapid technological advances in the midst of vast economic struggles leaves us all vulnerable to the effects of stress on our health and happiness. We can choose to be victims or assume that being stressed 24/7 is an unavoidable circumstance of life, but significant research indicates that this is not true. Some people are able to manage their stress in proactive ways by making use of their strengths. We can learn from such people and take responsibility for our own self-care.

This book is intended to be a reference and a hands-on practical guide to everyday stress management. It is an academic textbook that uses evidence-based research to support the information and tools provided. The purpose is not to provide an extensive review of all stress management tools, but rather, to offer pragmatic, student-tested tools to explore, experiment with, and make a part of everyday life.

This textbook first describes what happens to your health when you are under stress to help you appreciate the importance of making stress management part of your lifestyle, something you practice every day, or most days. Each dimension of wellness is then examined in relation to the detrimental effect of stress. Wellness is addressed from a holistic point of view and includes physical, emotional, intellectual, social, spiritual, and environmental dimensions. Because these dimensions of wellness affect each other, making a small change in one influences the others. For example, a change in your physical wellness as a result of exercise can "bleed into," or influence, your emotional wellness, resulting in your feeling less anxious and improving your mood.

I suggest that you hold on to this book after the completion of the course. Stress management, like many other wellness practices, has to be just that—practiced—every day! Some of the tools might appeal to you right now, whereas others might resonate later in your life, when you are working, parenting, starting a company, or even retiring. Growth and change are inevitable, and changing, modifying, and learning new stress management tools is one way to deal with these changes in healthy and positive ways.

Much of the evidence-based, scientific research presented in this book involved college students. The stress management techniques presented are grounded in experiential learning and have been tested on college students, who have offered suggestions for improvement. Several chapters feature discussion questions.

Instructors using this book will have access to an online instructor guide and test package. There they will find examples of a course syllabus, assignments, reproducibles, sample test questions, and discussion questions to supplement their teaching of the course. For students these materials and projects present opportunities to gain insight into their lives and what might be causing them stress. They also allow students the opportunity to explore and practice the stress-management tools found throughout this text.

Congratulations on taking the first step toward optimal wellness and happiness. In class you might be asked to move through the chapters sequentially, but you may also want to browse through the chapters on your own. If something catches your eye and you want to practice it—go for it! Good luck in your journey.

Namaste,
Nanette Tummers
Professor of health education
Eastern Connecticut State University
Willimantic, Connecticut

acknowledgments

I would not be an author without the dedicated and extraordinary professionals at Human Kinetics: Gayle Kassing, Cheri Scott, Anne Rumery, and special thanks to Ragen Sanner.

This book is dedicated to my best friend,
Leslie Clark. Thanks for all your inspiration.

Introduction to Stress and Stress Management

Your time is limited, so don't waste it living someone else's life. Don't be trapped by dogma—which is living with the results of other people's thinking. Don't let the noise of others' opinions drown out your own inner voice. And most important, have the courage to follow your heart and intuition. They somehow already know what you truly want to become. Everything else is secondary.

Steve Jobs' Stanford University Commencement Speech 2005

You may have never been taught how to take care of yourself in a positive and caring way. The skills of relaxation and focused concentration aren't often taught in higher education curriculums, but they are vital to learning and being healthy and happy now and in your future. For these reasons, this textbook is important.

The purpose of learning about stress and learning stress management tools is not to eliminate stress from your life. This is impossible. Stress is a natural response to change, and change is inevitable. Having a certain amount of stress in your life is normal. However, cumulative stress that results from excessive exposure to hassles, responsibilities, daily pressures, concerns, worries, and anger threatens our health and happiness.

The first step in dealing with stress is becoming aware of what stresses you and how your body reacts to it. Many of us have become experts at desensitizing ourselves or ignoring our bodies' signals. The question you have to ask yourself is this: Am I ready to take responsibility for paying attention to my stressors and how stress manifests in my life? Taking this first step will enhance your quality of life right now. Following are lists of the common symptoms of stress on various aspects of health:

Physical Symptoms of Stress

- Headaches and migraines
- Muscle tension
- Loss of appetite
- Cravings
- Indigestion, or gas, acid reflux, stomachaches
- Not wanting to be active
- Being accident prone
- Weight gain
- Weight loss
- Shortness of breath
- Feeling exhausted
- Sleeping a lot
- Having difficulty falling asleep or sustaining restful sleep
- Elevated blood pressure
- Cold hands
- Chest pain
- Lack of sex drive
- Jitters
- Diarrhea
- Constipation
- Racing heartbeat
- Extreme PMS
- Lethargy
- Disturbing dreams or nightmares
- New aches or pains
- Inability to shake off a cold
- Excessive eating
- Stress eating
- Jaw pain or grinding of teeth

Emotional Symptoms of Stress

- Rumination about or rehashing stressful memories
- Feeling defensive
- Crankiness
- Having difficulty remembering things
- Freezing or not being able to retrieve information
- Not being able to laugh or see the humor in situations
- Crying spells
- Change in voice tone
- Quick temper
- Racing thoughts
- Constant negative self-talk
- Depression
- Bad mood
- Feeling numb

Intellectual Symptoms of Stress

- Test anxiety
- Public speaking anxiety
- Having difficulty focusing
- Inability to prioritize
- Procrastination
- Making excuses, blaming
- Staring off into space; inability to focus
- Lack of motivation
- Irrational thoughts

Social Symptoms of Stress

- Shyness
- Aggressiveness
- Loss of voice
- Becoming violent or lashing out
- Feeling isolated or lonely
- Seeking isolation; not wanting to go out
- Passivity
- Having difficulty following a conversation
- Lowered desire for sex
- Inability to get organized
- Confusion
- Forgetfulness
- Pessimistic outlook
- Using others

Spiritual Symptoms of Stress

- Feeling hopeless or helpless
- Feeling powerless
- Lack of vision of the future
- Lack of interest in things that used to motivate or be enjoyable
- Focus on external gratification (e.g., gambling, pornography)
- Not having alone time

Environmental Symptoms of Stress

- Seasonal affective disorder
- Hearing loss
- Eye strain, headaches, back pain, carpal tunnel syndrome
- Asthma and respiratory problems
- Disorganization, clutter, unsafe or unhealthy living conditions
- Overspending, debt

You can find out more about symptoms of stress by viewing the website of the American Institute of Stress (AIS), a nonprofit organization that reports on the effects of stress, stress reduction methods, and various other stress-related topics: www.stress.org.

Wellness Versus Health

People often think of *health* in terms of its opposite (the absence of disease)—we feel "healthy" because we do not have symptoms of ill health such as a fever or stomachache. In the context of this book, *health* is used when referring to risk factors or symptoms of ill health or disease, such as smoking or poor nutrition (see the following description of the Western medical risk model). *Wellness* is focused on what we can do to increase our total well-being and optimize our everyday lives—this book's focus is on this wellness strengths-based approach. This means focusing on protective factors—those things we can do every day to protect and promote our wellness such as to seek out supportive friends or engage in physical activity.

The wellness strengths-based model conceptualized the health of the whole person to better understand both stress and stress management. We will use this model to examine stress in the context of optimal functioning in all six dimensions of wellness: physical, emotional, intellectual, social, spiritual, and environmental.

An important concept in the wellness model is the interrelationships among all the dimensions of wellness (see figure 1.1). To fully understand stress and stress management, we need to address all of these dimensions.

Most members of Western societies look primarily at the physical symptoms of stress without looking deeper at the causes, such as grieving from a loss or experiencing social isolation. For optimal well-being, you should investigate how much stress you experience in each wellness dimension, and practice as many wellness-based stress management tools as possible. The Western approach, or medical model, focuses on illness and disease and fixing these problems primarily through medications and surgery. The problem with using this approach with stress, such as taking medication, is that the medication may temporarily alleviate the symptoms brought on by the stressor, but it doesn't address the source of the stress. In other words, the problem doesn't go away.

Focus of the Western Medical Risk Model

- Blood pressure
- Heart rate
- Body composition
- Blood lipid (fat) levels
- Insulin sensitivity
- Hours of sleep
- Level of exercise
- Smoking
- Alcohol consumption
- Nutritional intake: sodium, fiber, fat, sugar
- Water intake
- Prescription and over-the-counter medication and supplement intake
- Drug abuse: illegal, prescription, over the counter
- Pain management
- Range of motion (flexibility) in major joints
- Core strength: abdominal and back muscles

Focus of the Wellness Strengths-Based Model

- Enjoyable physical activity
- Active lifestyle
- Emotional intelligence including empathy
- Meditation or prayer
- Use of relaxation techniques
- Meaningful work or volunteer time
- Optimism, happiness
- Social support
- Connectedness
- Spiritual expression
- Environmental engagement (e.g., green practices)
- Time outdoors
- Consumption of healthy foods in moderation
- Quiet time alone
- Restful, restorative sleep
- Positive self-talk
- Intellectual engagement
- Mindfulness
- Sense of humor
- Responsible self-management of time and finances
- Responsible self-management of alcohol and other substances and sexual activity
- Healthy weight management

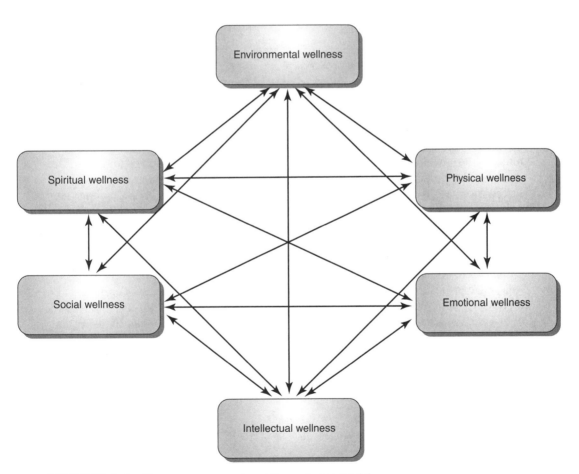

FIGURE 1.1   Stress management and the wellness model.

Researchers in the field of stress and stress management typically use the linear medical model of A causes B. They speculate on the reasons physical activity is such a successful stress management tool by asking this question: Is it the result of the social support experienced when playing basketball with friends, the physical release of endorphins that make people feel better, the satisfaction of accomplishing a goal such as running a 10K, improved mood, or the increase of oxygenated blood to the brain? However, the reasons for the benefits of physical activity on stress cannot be attributed to just one theory.

The most commonly prescribed medications (antidepressants, anti-anxiety medications, sleeping aids, and blood pressure and gastrointestinal medications) treat symptoms but do not address the underlying causes, which are often reactions to stress. For this reason, we must all develop our own stress management toolboxes. We can let stress get the better of us, or we can make the commitment to use stress management tools.

The concept of *locus of control* is helpful here. When we have an external locus of control, we let situations or other people dictate how we react to stress; we seek things outside of ourselves to blame for our problems or to make us feel better. This can lead to an attitude of helplessness or hopelessness. When we have an internal locus of control, we control our actions; we take responsibility for how we respond.

Good Stress Versus Not-So-Good Stress

There is such a thing as good, or positive, stress, which is known as *eustress*. This kind of stress can motivate us to make changes so we can meet challenges. As a response to eustress, we rise to the occasion by, for example, playing our best game or enjoying solving a math equation. As you will learn in this chapter, the key to being on top of our game and doing amazing things is perceiving the challenge in a positive light. Conversely, when we perceive stress as bad, it is called *distress*. As a reaction to distress, we can become upset, out of sorts, flipped out. When this happens, we are not using the higher-order thinking part of the brain—the prefrontal cortex—where our logical and creative power resides. Research has shown that during meditation (a stress management tool), the left prefrontal cortex becomes more active, which is associated with happiness and well-being. The brain actually gets stronger and larger as a result of meditation—it is like a workout for the brain (Lazar et al., 2005)!

Figure 1.2 shows the relationship between eustress or distress and performance, which is known as the inverted-U, or Yerkes-Dodson law (Yerkes & Dodson, 1908). This law can be applied to many situations in which performance is enhanced or decreased as a result of the perception of the stressor. We need stress to pump us up or get us psyched. Without a challenge, we would not be compelled to get up and take action. Without challenges, we get bored, procrastinate, and become apathetic and lazy. If the challenge is too overwhelming, however, we do not perform well

@ WEB LINK

Assess Individual Wellness

Lifescan Health Risk Appraisal. This online tool developed by Bill Hettler, cofounder of the National Wellness Institute at the University of Wisconsin at Stevens Point, can be used daily to assess individual wellness. http://wellness. uwsp.edu/other/lifescan

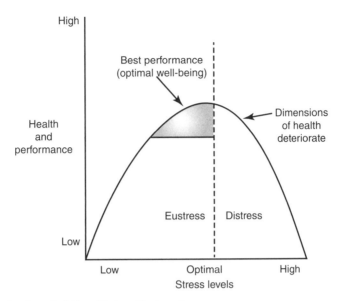

FIGURE 1.2   Inverted-U, or Yerkes-Dodson law.

because we are anxious. For example, we may choke at a very simple movement or a sport play we had previously performed without mistakes.

Distress can be a thought of like an honest friend—telling us when something isn't right and encouraging us to take the time to figure it out. The sense of something not being "right" is the body and mind gearing up for protection against a challenge.

When we think about stress, we mostly think of distress, or the not-so-good variety. Often, stress is a reaction not to a physical threat but to our ego or our sense of self. For example, we may feel our sense of self threatened when we have to speak in public or take a test, or are being disrespected—all of these are threats to who we believe we are. Instinctively, we react to this threat without thinking the situation through. Here is where we use the quick-and-dirty lower level of our brain known as the limbic system, which is closely tied to emotions, and the lowest part of the brain, the reptilian brain, which acts purely out of an instinct to survive.

The part of the brain's limbic system known as the *amygdala* is located in the brain stem. Its role is the regulation of emotions: generating and storing them, as well as connecting emotions to situations. In stressful situations, the amygdala can quickly override thinking and allow emotions to rule over the facts. To keep this from happening, we need to make a conscious, deliberate choice to stop in the moment just before the amygdala takes over. In her work in underserved schools in the San Francisco Bay Area, Amy Saltzman (n.d.) calls this moment "the almost moment." In stress management, we practice stopping at this critical juncture and shifting from emotion mode into a better thinking mode. In stress management, we *respond* to difficult thoughts and feelings rather than *react* when these thoughts and feelings take over.

Many Eastern philosophies advocate for finding the *middle path* for optimal performance and health. This refers to the "sweet spot" of making just enough

The most important organ in dealing with stress is the mind!

effort to meet the challenge. The fable of Goldilocks comes to mind: When we take on too much, we get frustrated; when we take on too little, we become bored and unmotivated. This textbook will help you find that middle path.

Stress management can be thought of as setting boundaries regarding our own sense of self, our energy, our relationships, and our health and safety. The purpose of this text is to describe ways to maintain healthy boundaries, increase protective factors, and decrease the use of unhealthy coping behaviors that put your health at risk.

Definitions of Stress

Several definitions of stress are used in today's society, which can be confusing. For the purpose of clarity, the following definitions will be used throughout this text:

- Stressor—The cause of stress; for example, final exams, a job interview, relationships.
- Stress reactivity—How people individually react to stressors.
- Stress symptoms—The effects on the body of stress reactivity; for example, headache, upset stomach.

Following are other important terms related to stress:

- Allostasis—The body's constant goal of maintaining equilibrium and balance during change (McEwen & Lasley, 2002).
- Allostatic load—The physiological burden on the body brought on by stress reactivity to continued physical, emotional, intellectual, social, spiritual, or environmental stressors. When stress reactivity continues unresolved, wear and tear on the body's systems make it difficult to repair and defend against illness, which can result in disease (McEwen & Lasley, 2002).
- Acute stress reactivity—The immediate reaction to a stressor. When the stressor is removed, the stress response ends.
- Tolerable stress—A level of stress that allows us to get back into balance, or allostasis, without excessive health costs.
- Toxic stress reactivity—The result of ongoing chronic, unrelenting stress that keeps the body in constant stress reactivity with subsequent harmful health effects.
- Sympathetic nervous system activation—The fight or flight response that causes the body to react to a threat to survival to protect itself from harm. This catabolic system breaks down complex nutrients to simple forms that the body can use easily.
- Parasympathetic nervous systems activation—The stimulation of the vagal nerve after the fight or flight response is over to bring about allostasis, or the return of the body to balance. This anabolic system is also known as "rest and digest" for its ability to build resistance and restore reserves.

Stress can be difficult to define and research not only because of its many definitions, but also because of the numerous theories of why and how much stress affects us. Theories of how individuals cope with stress address genetics as well as social and cultural factors. For example, we may inherit a proclivity to react strongly to stress from our parents (nature), but how that genetic proclivity is expressed may be affected by how we are taught to manage stress within our family and culture (nurture). Another theory addresses how exposure to significant stressful life events brings on stress reactivity. This text focuses on a strengths-based approach to stress management.

Stress and the Life Stage of Becoming an Adult

Life stages are critical passages of time that people go through. Each life stage has challenges that people need to experience and grow from. For example, adolescence is a stage in which people start to feel a sense of autonomy and challenge their parents' ideas. The life stage of young adulthood has unique challenges that can be sources of significant stress.

Stressors Faced by College Students

- Academics and decisions about a future career: major selection, courses, workload, deadlines, time management
- Academic difficulties such as poor study and test-taking skills; learning issues such as dyslexia and attention disorders
- Financial concerns: attaining scholarships, loans, budgeting
- Work: maintaining a job while in school
- Social relationships and intimate partner relationships
- Discrimination
- Future role in society, career
- Concern about the world situations: terrorism, politics, economics, workforce
- Independence, self-responsibility, and autonomy: parents too involved; roommate issues; living away from home
- Mental health issues such as depression, anxiety, addictive behaviors, and eating disorders
- Sexual identity and orientation, sexual issues
- Body image
- Commuting and living at home
- Lack of time to be alone and quiet
- Technology issues such as losing one's phone or one's computer crashing
- Being "on" and available 24/7, constantly checking one's phone so as not to miss out on something important
- Use of leisure time: finding a balance between downtime and other responsibilities
- Lifestyle issues: lack of sleep, partying, inactivity, poor nutrition, smoking, alcohol consumption
- Procrastination, lack of motivation, apathy

According to a report from the American Psychological Association titled "Stress in America: Our Health at Risk" (2012), people 18 to 32 years old (known as the Millennials) reported the following sources of stress:

- Money (80 percent)
- Work (72 percent)

Adjusting to the responsibilities and pressures of adulthood can be stressful for many people.

- Cost of housing (49 percent)
- Economy (54 percent)
- Nervous or anxious as a result of stress in the past month (45 percent)

Almost 60 percent of respondents considered stress management to be important, but only 32 percent believed that they were very good or excellent at dealing with stress. This is a textbook that can help!

According to the American Psychological Association (n.d.a), anxiety and feeling down often occur together in college students. However, in depression, these symptoms tend to last longer than just feeling the blues. Symptoms of depression include lack of interest and pleasure in previously enjoyable activities or everyday activities, significant changes in weight, sleep disruptions including insomnia or excessive sleeping, lethargy, difficulty concentrating, feeling hopeless, helplessness or low self-worth, and consistent thoughts of death or suicide. If you are exhibiting any or all of these symptoms, you should see a counselor. Also, urge a friend with these symptoms to see a counselor. Find out about your campus mental health and counseling resources.

Understanding the Stress Response: Fight or Flight

Our genes carry a survival mechanism that has worked for thousands of years. This innate response to the perception of being threatened is what propels our bodies into either fighting or fleeing—as if the situation were a matter of life or death. This response has kept our DNA intact. When our ancestors were confronted by physical danger—being attacked by an enemy or about to become someone's lunch—they fought or escaped. After the threat was over, they probably slept it off, replenished their systems, and returned to allostasis.

The problem is that evolution has not caught up with the unique stressors of this super-fast and changing technological age. Most of our stressors today are internal; that is, they are a threat to our sense of self. Our world is very stressful and uncertain. Although we may not be in direct contact with stressful events, we still feel the fallout from information overload every time we watch TV or read a news clip on our iPads. The fight or flight response doesn't help because we can't run away from a trigonometry test; we have to sit and stew away in our frustration. And we can't physically kick someone's behind if that person is stressing us.

One of the first researchers of stress, Hans Selye, investigated the effect of stress on mice (1970). In his laboratory he observed that mice under long-term stress became sick—from stomach ulcers, inflamed adrenal glands, and suppressed immune cells. Selye found that animals followed a pattern. Reacting to the stressor activated the fight or flight response, what he called the alarm phase. If the stressor continued, the animal actually adapted and became resistant to the stressor; Selye termed this the resistance phase. However, the amount of resistance mice can endure is limited, and the mice eventually succumbed to the exhaustion phase. Mice who were not allowed to rest and recover died. During final exams, students may feel that they are more effective at studying when they stay up all night (i.e., put up resistance to the stressor), but they typically reap the negative effects of exhaustion afterward, such as illness. This phase is known as *allostatic load*—allostatic load is the consequence, in body wear and tear, of chronic exposure to stress (McEwen, 2005).

When the body is in fight or flight mode, or stress reactivity, the immediate needs of the body are the chief concern. Blood is diverted to the muscles and away from the digestive and reproductive systems. The needs of the immune, digestion, and reproduction systems are put on the back burner. If the stress continues over a prolonged period of time (i.e., toxic stress reactivity), these systems become compromised. For example, the production of white cells and other immune cells decreases, digestion suffers, and sexual health issues such as PMS, hot flashes, and impotence can occur.

What Happens During Stress Reactivity or the Stress Response

The body uses a system of chemical messengers that are made up of proteins called neuropeptides. Although this system is regulated by the brain, these messengers can also be released from other parts of the body such as the immune system or the digestive system. Our bodies react to either a physical threat or a threat to our self-perception. Consider the constantly recurring message that we are unlovable after a relationship breakup. Our bodies keep kicking out these messengers, going through the same reactions over and over.

Following are immediate stress reactions:

- Heart rate, breathing rate, and blood pressure increase to deliver oxygenated and nutrient-rich blood to working muscles to take action against the threat.
- Stress hormones are released into the bloodstream: epinephrine, norepinephrine, cortisol.
- The liver releases stored glycogen to be converted to glucose to provide energy for the actions of fighting or fleeing.
- The pupils dilate to see better.
- The lungs take in more oxygen through increased respiration.
- Muscles tense in preparation for muscle contractions, which are fueled by the release of glucose into the bloodstream.
- Blood flow is increased to large muscles with decreased flow to digestive and reproductive organs and periphery (hands and feet).
- Sweat increases to cool the body from increased metabolism.
- Blood thickens to facilitate clotting so any wounds incurred won't bleed out.

- Immune cells are mobilized in case of a wound or infection.
- Hair follicles become erect to make the person appear bigger or more dangerous.

If the danger or threat ends, the body goes into equilibrium mode to come back to allostasis. But what happens if the fight or flight response continues in reaction to a stressor that is not life threatening? In this case the body starts to run down like a cell phone battery and is vulnerable at its weakest link. The excessive use of caffeine, a lack of sleep, a lack of exercise, and poor eating habits can compound the problem.

Let's go into more detail of exactly what happens systemically during stress reactivity. Figure 1.3 will help you visualize the stress response.

When a person is under stress, information from the sensory organs (e.g., the eyes see snakes) is relayed to the hypothalamus (in the brain) for an immediate response. The brain responds to what it perceives to be a threat and sends information via nerve impulses to the sympathetic branch of the autonomic nervous system. The sympathetic branch first energizes the muscular system, telling the person that it's time to fight or get the heck out of there. The autonomic nervous system also is stimulated to activate the involuntary, or automatic, processes such as increasing heart rate and blood pressure.

If the threat continues (e.g., the snakes are getting closer and there are more of them), the hormonal system comes into play. This system takes longer to kick into full gear because the hormones must travel through the circulatory system. The hypothalamus and the pituitary glands (both in the brain) release hormones (chemical messengers) that cause a multitude of reactions. The hypothalamus releases endorphins, powerful painkillers, in anticipation of injury or pain from fighting or fleeing. The hormones epinephrine and norepinephrine (also known by the lay term *adrenaline*) are also released and are responsible for an increase in breathing rate, heart rate, and blood pressure and the release of glucose to increase the amount of oxygen and fuel (sugar or glucose) in the blood that is delivered to the working muscles.

To meet the demand for the fuel needed for fighting and fleeing, fat and cholesterol are released into the bloodstream as well. Keep in mind, however, that the body responds with the same patterns whether the person is being chased by a pit bull or taking a test. If the fat and cholesterol are not used for energy, they must be stored and are often deposited in the abdominal area and in the blood vessels.

As the stressor continues, the hypothalamus releases another hormone called *corticotrophin releasing factor (CRF)*, a key chemical in setting off the domino effect of the stress response. CRF signals the pituitary gland to release another hormone called *adrenocorticotropic hormone (ACTH)*, which signals the adrenals glands to release cortisol, aldosterone, fibrogen, and more epinephrine. These chemicals protect the body from damage by increasing the circulation of immune cells to prevent infection at any potential wound site, and by thickening the blood so it can clot quickly in response to any wounds incurred during fighting or fleeing. Toxic stress reactivity occurs when the levels of these chemicals adversely affect immune cell activity, resulting in inflammation and the thickening of the blood, which can cause heart complications such as stroke or embolism (blood clot) (Bosma-den Boer, van Welten, & Priumboom, 2012).

During stress, the thyroid gland also releases hormones to accelerate metabolism so that blood sugar is released into the circulatory system. This releases the hormone insulin to regulate the blood sugar levels. Under prolonged stress, glucose and insulin levels can cause problems such as insulin resistance, diabetes, and metabolic syndrome.

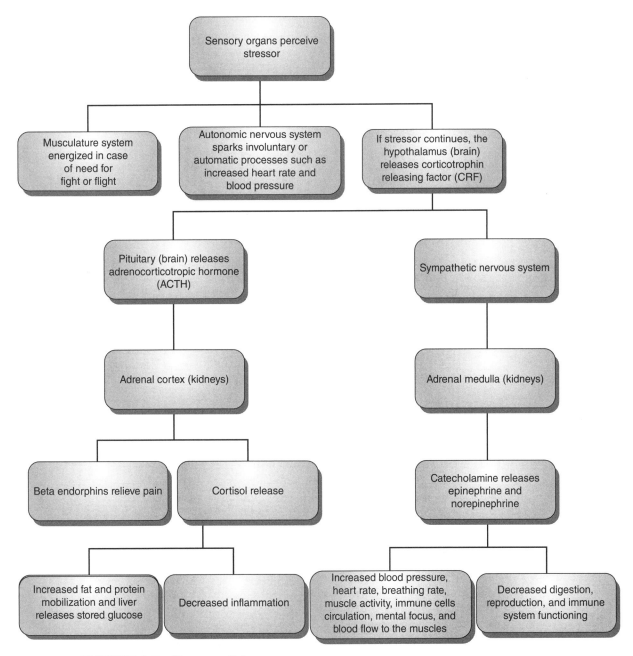

FIGURE 1.3 Stress reactivity.

Remember that the body cannot distinguish among an actual physical threat to existence, an imagined threat, and an emotional threat. Imagine that the snake you thought you saw turns out to be just a stick in the road. You can laugh off your mistaken perception and hope that no one saw your reaction, and you may feel a sense of relief, but also fatigue. This is because your body has been through an enormous amount of activity, and this requires a lot of energy!

Following the stress response, the other branch of the autonomic nervous system comes into play—the parasympathetic nervous system. This system is known as the rest and digest system; its role is to bring the body back to normal levels of functioning through such actions as lowering blood pressure and decreasing the breathing rate. This process, as mentioned previously, is called allostasis.

When the stress is over and the body is returning to balance, or allostasis, the cortisol and other hormones are not immediately removed from the system. The half-life (i.e., the amount of time required to be reduced to 50 percent of the pre-stress dose) of epinephrine and norepinephrine is one to three minutes, but the half-life of cortisol is over 60 minutes. The continued presence of cortisol signals an increase in appetite to replace the glucose and fat that should have been used during the physical exertion of fighting or fleeing. The body craves more fat and carbohydrate to replace its stores so it will function optimally when confronting future threats to survival. The problem is that the body does all this with the assumption that the stressor was a physical threat requiring fuel, rather than, say, an emotional threat of being dumped by a romantic partner. Because all this energy has not been used up physically, the elevated amounts of glucose trigger the release of insulin to regulate these substrates. Cortisol is believed to be responsible for storing this excess energy as body fat, which tends to accumulate around the middle of the body close to the heart. This abdominal fat, or android fat, is considered a risk factor for heart disease. Cortisol also sends the liver into overdrive to manage the elevated cholesterol and fat levels in the blood, and it may also signal the body to "rest and digest" and become less active to conserve energy stores.

Scary Movies, Roller Coasters, Double Black Diamond Ski Runs

Regardless of whether a threat is a scary spider or just a piece of lint, the brain perceives the danger as real. The cerebral cortex produces the energizing neuro-transmitters glutamate, dopamine, and serotonin to intensify and strengthen the body to fight or flee from this danger. When we take the time to monitor our emotional response, the cerebral cortex has enough time to perceive the threat as just a piece of lint and stop the cascade of hormones. It releases gamma-aminobutyric acid (GABA), which produces a state of calm and a return to allostasis.

In the case of a fun challenge such as a roller coaster or a double black diamond ski run, the danger warning has already switched on the hypothalamus, the part of the brain that communicates with the adrenal glands to produce epinephrine. As a result, our senses become alive and sharp. This hormone switches on the release of beta-endorphin, which decreases pain and increases the pleasure response. We know we are in control, the stress response shuts down, and we perceive the situation as positive. This explains why we love this "rush" and seek it out through risk taking, exercise, and sexual activity.

When the body is under continued or chronic stress and is no longer able to provide resistance let alone return to allostasis, it becomes depleted and cannot rest and restore itself. Selye called this third stage exhaustion; it is the point at which the body succumbs to the allostatic load. Because the normal defenses for fighting off infection are not in place, the body is vulnerable to illness and disease. Allostatic load refers to the cumulative effect of chronic stress and the resulting exhaustion (McEwen, 2005).

Students often wonder whether they have been socially or culturally trained to be busy or are addicted to being stressed or busy 24/7. Some worry that if they took the time to practice stress management, they might be perceived by others as lazy or slackers. Keep in mind that the continued effect of stress reactivity takes its toll on brain functioning and learning as well as on all aspects of health. We all need to take steps to prevent our bodies from succumbing to allostatic load. We examine the pathophysiology of stress in the next section.

The Pathophysiology of Stress

The brain is the first line of defense when encountering a stressor. It reacts with a release of chemicals and hormones into the bloodstream so as to be sharp and immediately reactive to the perceived threat. However, this course of action is not without serious consequences. Chronically elevated levels of stress hormones can be toxic to brain cells and can cause nerve damage, memory loss, and impaired thinking. Prolonged exposure can damage the cells of the hippocampus, which impairs learning. Students report that they can become angry, fatigued, and depressed easily under prolonged stress.

According to Rossman (2010), a physician who has written extensively about anxiety and health, emotions are encoded into memory during a specific chemical state known as state-dependency (p. 62). When we are upset, it is difficult to connect to a state of calm and easier to snap to angry thoughts. In addition, in the upset or angry state, we may remember old hurts and emotions. To be our best intellectually, Rossman explained, we need to shift to a calmer state, which takes practice.

A modern phenomenon that would not have been a wise choice for our ancestors is ruminating about a situation rather than fighting it or fleeing from it. Continuously "chewing on" or "stewing about" a situation may lead to feelings of hopelessness, helplessness, and defeat. When stuck in stress reactivity, the body continues to release cortisol and epinephrine. Later chapters discuss research that shows how stress management tools such as meditation and reframing our thinking can help us get unstuck from ruminating and lead to enhanced brain functioning.

Elevated levels of the primary hormones of the endocrine system (epinephrine, norepinephrine, and cortisol) are linked to health complications such as heart problems, diabetes, and strokes. In the case of diabetes, although it can be treated with medication, diet, and physical activity, blood sugars are difficult to control when stress continues to trigger the release of sugar into the bloodstream. Stress management can be very helpful in the treatment of diabetes, which affects millions of adults worldwide (Morris, Moore, & Morris, 2011).

Stress reactivity causes an increase in blood pressure and heart rate, which puts a strain on and weakens the lining of blood vessels. This in turn causes inflammation, and the body responds by depositing fat in the lining, or endothelium, of the blood vessels. The elevated blood fats levels are carried through the bloodstream by lipoproteins. Foods that are high in saturated fat have high amounts of low-density lipoproteins, which cause inflammation and damage to this lining. This causes the artery already lined with plaque to further narrow, slowing circulation. Stress reactivity also causes the blood to thicken, resulting in more clots. Moreover, because circulation is slowed down in the arteries, the risk of spasms, pain, and heart complications, as well as strokes, increases because of the possibility of clots traveling to occlude other blood vessels.

The problem today is that our stressors, by their nature, do not provide an opportunity to use the emergency hormones released into our bodies through the physical exertion of fighting or fleeing. As a result, these hormones stay in the body and wreak havoc. Americans are some of the most sedentary, out of shape, and unhealthy people in the world. This is demonstrated by the increasing health problems associated with obesity—increased rates of diabetes and hyperlipidemia (elevated blood cholesterol). Physical activity helps to use up the excess energy released during stress. Additionally, during physical activity the body releases the hormones endorphin, serotonin, and dopamine, which positively affect thoughts and emotions. Research has shown that people who exercise regularly have lower levels of mild to moderate depression and anxiety. Researchers have also found that being subjected to long-term stress can deplete endorphin levels, which can result in aggravating the pain from headaches and back pain.

During the stress response, blood is shunted away from the core to the large muscles of the body—to the arm and leg muscles used to run or fight. However, our bodies need a great deal of energy to properly digest and metabolize food and make the resulting substrates available to the entire body for growth and repair and the replenishment of energy reserves. When the digestive and assimilation processes are interrupted by stress, the gastrointestinal tract suffers with complications such as irritable bowel syndrome (IBS). In children, the most often-cited health complaint is a tummy ache, which can be the start of a lifetime of gastrointestinal problems.

Stress decreases the body's ability to deal with chronic inflammation caused by increased cortisol levels, resulting in suppressed immune system activity. Most of the devastating diseases we face—including cardiovascular disease, diabetes, respiratory disease, autoimmune diseases, aggravated pain responses, and cancer—have been linked to the inflammation brought on by allostatic load and the body's inability to achieve allostasis (Bosma-den Boer et al., 2012; Morris et al., 2011; Wardle et al., 2011; Yusuf et al., 2004).

Stress can cause an overstimulation of muscle activity such as nervous tics or uncontrollable movement (e.g., hands shaking). It can also inhibit the muscles' ability to execute coordinated movements resulting in mistakes such as overreactions or compensations in stressful situations (e.g., oversteering a car or missing an easy basketball shot).

Because the skin is the largest sensory organ in the body, it is most vulnerable to the effects of stress. Research has linked the skin disorders of hives, rashes, acne, and eczema to anger. When someone is under stress, wounds do not heal quickly. In fact, patients going into surgery are often encouraged to practice stress management activities such as imagery to help their incisions to heal quickly and with less infection. This brings us to the important association between the mind and physical health.

The body also becomes vulnerable to microbes in the environment when under prolonged stress. The immune system is a network of organs, tissues, and white blood cells and other specialized cells whose role is to defend against diseases. Much of this system is regulated by the endocrine system, which uses specialized chemicals to communicate with the other systems. Under prolonged stress, elevated cortisol hinders the body's ability to produce and maintain lymphocytes—the white blood cells that fight off threats to the immune system.

To put it simply, when we are in chronic stress reactivity, we are depleted and our ability to heal and thrive is compromised. If you keep withdrawing from your bank account without depositing, you will run out of money; it's like that with your

@ WEB LINK

Pathophysiology of Stress

U.S. Centers for Disease Control and Prevention. This site offers updates on stress research. www.cdc.gov/vitalsigns

body—you need overdraft protection. This text will give you countless ways to augment your physical overdraft protection and improve your health and happiness.

Mind–Body Health: Psychoneuroimmunology

Herbert Benson, author of *The Relaxation Response* (2000), studied extensively the epidemic of hypertension and its roots in stress reactivity. He argued that stress reactivity damages every cell and every system of the body. His research revealed that many illnesses and diseases could be attributed to stress, including hypertension, asthma, bronchitis, amenorrhea, fertility problems, loss of libido, insulin resistance, and osteoporosis. He contended that our system of medicine is too dependent on medication and surgery and not enough on "self-care"—his term for the innate ability to bring about our own "healing and rejuvenation" (p. xvii). Self-care puts the control within the individual—emphasizing again the importance of an internal locus of control.

Benson was one of the early advocates of the U.S. government's establishing the National Center for Complementary and Alternative Medicine (NCCAM) as a branch of the National Institutes of Health (Benson, 2000). The term *integrative medicine* is used to describe a combination of conventional and complementary and alternative treatments (CAM). NCCAM supports CAM research and funds studies investigating topics ranging from melatonin for sleep disorders to yoga for low back pain (see figure 1.4). More and more Americans are using CAM treatments and are paying out of their pockets for these services and products (see figure 1.5).

The link between stress and disease is becoming stronger in the scientific literature. This has led to the identification of many "lifestyle diseases" such as heart disease and cancer, which have been linked to health behaviors such as smoking and inactivity. The term *lifestyle* refers to habitual behaviors, many of which are intricately linked to stress. For example, someone under stress at work might smoke

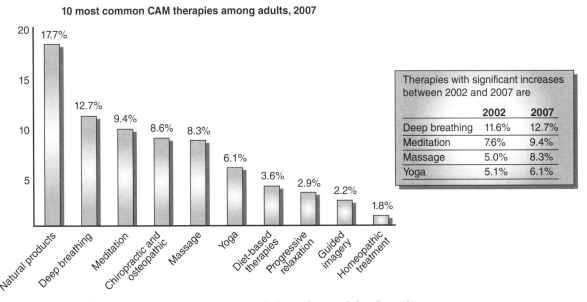

FIGURE 1.4 Most common complementary and alternative medicine therapies.

National Center for Complementary and Alternative Medicine 2007.

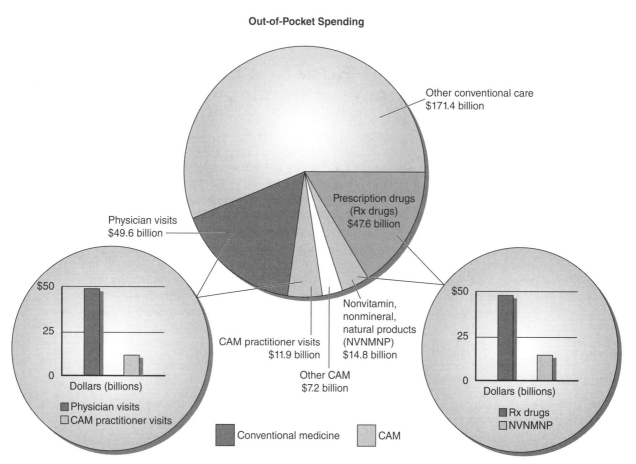

FIGURE 1.5 Out-of-pocket expenses spent on CAM therapies (not covered by insurance).

National Center for Complementary and Alternative Medicine 2011.

or drink alcohol to excess. The perception may be that lifestyle diseases manifest only in adulthood, but more and more college students are suffering from the ill effects of unhealthy lifestyle practices such as inadequate sleep, substance abuse, and inactivity.

Researchers have estimated that 50 to 90 percent of illness is tied to stress reactivity. Prolonged stress reactivity can cause deregulation or a malfunction as a result of an overresponsive sympathetic nervous system. Allergic reactions, exaggerated inflammation responses in rheumatoid arthritis, or an underresponsive or suppressed immune system, for example, make fighting off viruses and infections more difficult.

In the emerging field of *psychoneuroimmunology*, or PNI, scientists have demonstrated the relationships among the psyche, the nervous system, and the immune system.

P: The cognitive perceptions at the brain level, or **psyche**, such as negative thinking or anger, as well as prayer and optimism

N: The activation of the **nervous** system to relay messages to and from the other systems of the body including the endocrine system. The nervous system innervates the thymus, spleen, lymph system, and bone marrow. All of these organs and tissues are part of the immune system.

I: The **immune** system's job is to protect against infection and to produce cells to fight off illness. The battle starts in the white blood cells, which fight off foreign invaders.

Once the brain sends a message to the nervous system that the person is under threat, the nervous system then starts sending out emergency, or fight or flight, messengers (hormones). All the body cares about is preserving itself against this threat in this moment and not the long term. The immune system is put aside because diseases and illness are just not important when the person could be someone else's lunch. The body has to prioritize. These emergency chemicals wreak havoc on the immune system, sending it into a tailspin and often resulting in illness or disease (Pelletier & Herzing, 1988). Chronic stress drains the immune system's defenses, making the body vulnerable to any bacteria or viruses that come along. A healthy immune system can immobilize most foreign invaders. Students often come down with viral infections such as the flu or upper respiratory infections during periods of prolonged stress (e.g., final exam week).

Placebo Effect

An important area of psychoneuroimmunology (PNI), and part of any research study, is the *placebo effect*—a physical effect caused by a belief in the effectiveness of a treatment or procedure. The classic demonstration of this effect is treating pain patients with a sugar pill or fake treatment. When neither the researchers nor the patients know which patients are getting the actual pain medication and which are getting the fake one, this is known as a double blind study. The belief in pain relief actually stimulates the release of endorphins—the body's natural pain-relieving hormone. The placebo effect is so important in pharmaceutical research that it must be factored in when making claims about the efficacy of any drug; in fact, this effect can account for up to 35 percent of a drug's effectiveness.

The placebo effect demonstrates the power of the mind to make us happier and healthier. A belief in healing, prayer, relaxation, meditation—these are all powerful tools that promote health and stress management. Many athletes use creative imagination to improve their performance; they imagine themselves throwing the perfect pitch or free throw (see chapter 4 for a more in-depth discussion of creative imagination). Children who have cancer and imagine an action hero rounding up and destroying cancer cells actually improve their white blood cells counts. Surgical patients who imagine their wounds healing often heal faster and without infection and other postsurgical complications.

@ WEB LINKS

Medicine and Stress

- National Center for Complementary and Alternative Medicine (NCCAM). NCCAM is part of the National Institutes of Health and funds scientific research on complementary and alternative medicine. Its website provides summaries of research already completed and information on upcoming research and opportunities to be included in clinical trials. http://nccam.nih.gov/research
- National Institutes of Health (NIH). The NIH website includes a discussion of stress. www.nlm.nih.gov/medlineplus/stress.html

Strengths-Based Approach

We often look to the medical model to help us deal with the effects of stress. Medicines such as aspirin and anti-anxiety medications, however, treat the symptoms of stress but do not address the problem itself. It is up to each of us to develop our own stress management toolbox and to choose to respond to stress with these tools. When, instead, we habitually choose to be fearful, we feel helpless and unable to cope. We have the power to change this habit of being fearful and insecure, worrying all the time, being anxious and on edge.

A strengths-based approach to stress management enables us to be proactive in managing stress. Instead of focusing on what not do (e.g., have an angry outburst or self-medicate by drinking excessive amounts of alcohol), this approach focuses on health-enhancing practices such as being optimistic, believing in our abilities, increasing our happiness and motivation, and tapping into our unique intelligences.

Well-Being

Martin Seligman is considered a pioneer in the field of positive psychology. He used the term *flourish* to indicate a state of positive mental and social well-being (Seligman, 2011). Seligman's "well-being theory" addresses positive emotion, engagement, meaning, positive relationship, and accomplishment (2011, p. 12). This section explores in depth the qualities of well-being, or the strengths-based approach.

When people believe in their ability to make changes and take action, they have a sense of self-efficacy, a belief in their strengths (Bandura, 1986). To build your strengths, you must investigate your perception, or locus, of control. As mentioned earlier in this chapter, having an internal locus of control means being able to tap into and use your strengths.

Seligman and colleagues also developed the concept of *learned helplessness* (2007). People who show a lack of motivation, distort situations, and use being helpless to get others to step up and do the work for them or to excuse themselves from expectations are said to be in a state of learned helplessness. Such people clearly have an external locus of control. An example of learned helplessness is a student who uses a past illness as an excuse to not hand in work on time because she has "learned" that she can get away with this behavior.

Seligman and colleagues went on to develop a construct called *learned optimism*. Helplessness and optimism are not inherited, but rather, are learned behaviors. In other words, optimism can be taught. People's levels of optimism are rooted in their locus of control. They perceive and explain their locus of control through what Seligman termed their *explanatory style* (see table 1.1). Explanatory style includes three aspects:

- How much responsibility the person takes for the situation
- How much responsibility the person assigns to others
- How much the person attributes the situation to luck or chance

TABLE 1.1   Optimistic and Pessimistic Explanatory Styles

Optimistic explanatory style	Pessimistic explanatory style
This situation is just one bump in the road; it is temporary. The situation itself may not be completely within my control, but how I react to it is.	This situation is permanent and is the way it always is—pervasive. Nothing I ever do is right for anyone; this always happens to me.

People facing a difficult situation who focus on their ability to take responsibility have an internal locus of control. Those with an external locus of control assign responsibility for the outcomes of the situation to someone or something else—"the professor is having a bad day," or "people just don't like me," or fate, or chance. When we hang on to limited and pessimistic thinking, it becomes who we are and our reality. If we continue to feed these negative thoughts, they become self-limiting beliefs and self-fulfilling prophecies (e.g., "I am too stupid to do that," or "I am too slow"). Putting the blame on others leaves very little room to make the situation better, which can lead to feeling helpless and a victim. Rene Descartes, the French philosopher, summed this concept up well when he said, "I think, therefore I am." The play on this, "I think, therefore I suffer," is equally apt.

Did you know that the symbols in Chinese for stress mean that we are so busy that we forget our heart and mind? CenterTao.org

Hierarchy of Motivation

Abraham Maslow was one of the first to study the positive characteristics of people who had weathered adverse circumstances—specifically during World War II. He called this a "humanistic approach" to understanding people's needs and motivations (see figure 1.6). Maslow described a hierarchy of needs from the basic level of physiological needs such as food and shelter. His premise was that basic needs must be fulfilled before we can move on to fulfilling higher-level needs. The highest need is for transcendence to a higher self.

Fulfilling basic physiological needs is certainly imperative, although we can become too focused on external needs such as clothes, living spaces, and cars. At some point we need to move toward higher-level, inner needs such as love, compassion, and connectedness. External needs cannot substitute for these internal needs.

Maslow's hierarchy is the foundation for many of the subsequent models of a strengths-based wellness approach. His research on the characteristics of motivation relates directly to the concepts of hardiness and resilience (2011). Maslow also found creativity to be an important skill for dealing with change. The ability to think outside of ruts and to learn from mistakes motivates people to perceive challenges as opportunities.

Multiple Intelligences

Howard Gardner provided another perspective related to developing our strengths and fulfilling our highest potential. Instead of looking at our weaknesses, he suggested that we seek opportunities to improve our innate intelligence (1983). Many

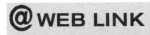 **WEB LINK**

Positive Psychology

Positive Psychology Center. Positive psychology research investigates strengths-based approaches that allow people to flourish. The Positive Psychology Center is housed at the University of Pennsylvania and promotes scientific research, training, and education. www.positivepsychology.org

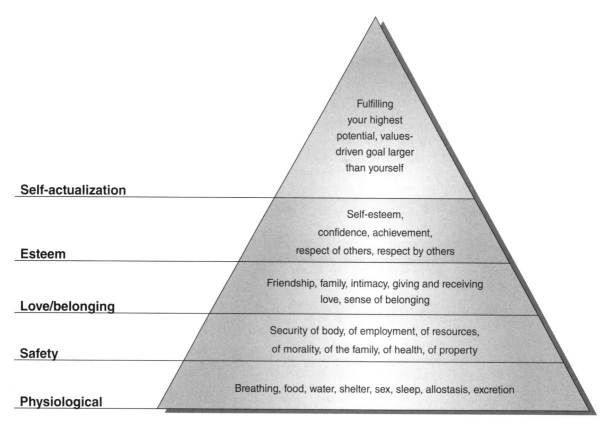

FIGURE 1.6   Maslow's hierarchy of needs.

Adapted from Finkelstein 2006.

who hear the word *intelligence* automatically think of intellectual intelligence. Gardner suggested that intelligence is multifaceted and includes the following:

- Music intelligence
- Visual-spatial intelligence
- Logistics and mathematical intelligence
- Verbal and linguistics intelligence
- Naturalistic intelligence
- Body intelligence
- Self-knowledge
- Social intelligence

For example, a person who is a whiz at math but can't work with people and communicate may have difficulty finding a job. This text offers numerous ideas for improving each area of intelligence. This approach challenges you to get out of your rut of doing what you always do to manage your stress and instead try something that strengthens another area of intelligence. For example, if you are not very athletic, trying some of the physical activities known to decrease stress, such as yoga and tai chi, can improve your kinesthetic intelligence.

We tend to focus on negative behaviors that contribute to and amplify our stress symptoms such as pessimism, hopelessness, defeatism, anger, and aggression. This book examines people facing similar stressors to yours, and perhaps even stressors worse than any one of us could imagine, and yet remained healthy and happy. What do these people have going for them, and how can we get some?

The reason for a holistic approach to stress management is to go beyond the symptoms to a deeper understanding of the problem, and then to develop the strengths to deal with the problem proactively. Imagine that you have to give an oral presentation in class. To decrease your stress level before the event, you have a few beers to loosen up; but now you have to deal with the possible consequences of this choice such as drunk driving. Better choices would be to examine your self-talk, use affirmations, plan your time, rehearse with flash cards, get a friend to listen to your presentation, practice deep breathing, and use creative imagination before the presentation. These action help you take control of the situation, and represent a skill set you can use over and over again.

Negative coping skills or ways to deal with stress include drinking, overeating, and getting into arguments. This text focuses on positive coping skills. Keep in mind, however, that positive coping skills can change to negative. For example, an exercise regime to manage stress can become a negative means of coping if it is done compulsively or excessively.

Hardiness

People who view change as a necessary and vital part of life are considered to be hardy. Suzanne Kobasa (1979) at the University of Chicago researched workers suffering from a massive layoff (not an uncommon event in today's economy). She found three consistent characteristics in those who weathered the storm of stress and uncertainty and termed this *hardiness*:

- *Challenge.* Perceiving a situation as a challenge fuels creativity and increases one's motivation to meet it. Part of the characteristic of challenge is what is called *compensation*, which is the ability to focus on strengths rather than weaknesses and engage one's personal sense of responsibility.

- *Commitment.* Sticking with one's goals and striving for one's highest potential describes commitment. Committed people have an intention to be part of the solution and not the problem; they believe that their efforts will result in things working out for the best.

- *Control.* The ability to do all one can within one's power is a definition of control.

Kobasa (1979) found that hardiness can be increased by two strategies: self-improvement and reconstructing past stressful events. Self-improvement means focusing on what we can control and putting our energies and focus into positive actions. Reconstructing the stressful event involves reframing our skewed perceptions of it and imagining responding with constructive actions next time.

Flow

Mihaly Csikszentmihalyi coined the term *flow* to describe the experience of being passionately immersed and totally engaged in a challenging activity without attachment to the outcome, to time, or to one's performance (1997). Csikszentmihalyi discovered that intrinsic motivation increases when an activity such as work becomes more like play—that is, something the person would continue to do it without reward. Csikszentmihalyi's concept of flow resonates with another strengths attribute called mindfulness, which is a state of being in the present moment with full attention and without attachment or expectations. Mindfulness is discussed in greater detail in chapter 4. Can you find things to do every day to make you feel in a state of flow? Doing a hobby, performing some physical activity, cooking, creating something without expectations about the results—it is what Nike's slogan says: Just do it!

Serenity Prayer

This prayer may make you think of the 12-step program, but it has been around for a long time. Think of it as a mantra to help you focus on your choices, on your locus of control.

Grant me the serenity to accept the things I cannot change, the courage to change the things I can, and the wisdom to know the difference.

Attributed to Reinhold Niebuhr

Resilience

Resilience is the ability to adapt and be healthy in spite of stressful and aversive circumstances. How resilient we are in the face of stressors has a lot to do with how we assess or perceive and subsequently cope with life events. Researchers led by Karen Reivich (Reivich & Shatte, 2002) at the University of Pennsylvania found the following qualities in resilient people:

- Self-efficacy—A belief in the ability to steer through difficult times.
- Emotional regulation—The ability to stay calm during stressful situations.
- Impulse control—The ability to respond in a controlled manner rather than act out in a compulsive way.
- Empathy—The capacity to recognize emotions in others.
- Optimism—The ability to see situations and future outcomes in a positive light.
- Reaching out to others—A sense of connectedness results in a strong base of social support.
- Problem solving and learning from setbacks—An ability to analyze and solve problems and learn from setbacks.

We can all improve our resilience; this text provides pragmatic and concrete ways to improve this and other strengths.

Positivity

Barbara Fredrickson, Kenan Distinguished Professor of Psychology at the University of North Carolina at Chapel Hill, provides substantial evidence to support a strengths-based approach to health. In her book *Positivity* (2009), Fredrickson discovered the connection between being positive and open-minded in learning, the ability to cope, and relationships with improvements in health. She recommends a ratio of 3 to 1—that is, for every negative emotional experience, or downer, people should have at least three positive emotional experiences, or lifters. Negativity can never be eliminated, but a lot of negativity results from having rigid expectations. Negativity can be simply a habit such as stewing over being wronged or jumping to conclusions. Fredrickson offers 10 forms of positivity:

- Joy
- Interest

- Amusement
- Love
- Gratitude
- Pride
- Awe
- Hope
- Inspiration
- Serenity

Take the positivity self-test to determine your ratio of positive emotions to negative emotions developed by Barbara Fredrickson (www.positivityratio.com).

Journaling

Journaling is the practice of documenting personal feelings, thoughts, and perceptions in writing. Journals have been used throughout history to process personal issues. Writing can serve the following functions:

- To release toxic emotions (as a catharsis)
- To increase awareness, accountability, and ownership
- To view situations with detachment and objectivity

Establishing a journaling ritual can increase the benefits of the writing experience. Such a ritual can include the following:

Stay open to the positive in all aspects of your life by aiming to keep your focus on positivity with a 3-to-1 ratio of positive-to-negative experiences. This way you focus on things like joy, love, and gratitude in your life instead of more negative emotions.

- A breathing or centering activity
- Setting an affirmation to be authentic, honest, spontaneous, uncensored
- Using a designated journal
- Seeking out a quiet environment where you won't be interrupted
- If writing is difficult, including doodles, sketches, or images
- Setting a timer when writing (15 to 20 minutes is optimal)

Resist the temptation to use a word processor on a computer when journaling. Give yourself the time necessary for the slower physical practice of writing your thoughts, emotions, and feelings by hand.

EXPLORING VALUES

Values are factors that make living purposeful. We often feel stressed because we get overwhelmed and exhausted and do not have the energy to enjoy what we value. Meanwhile, values are the most important things in our lives. They make us want to wake up each day.

- Brainstorm all the things you value—for example, education, friendships, freedom, and creativity.
- Reflect on ways you could spend more time with the things and people you value.
- Discuss how stress interferes with pursuing or enjoying your values.
- Discuss how stress management could strengthen your values.

A JOURNEY BEGINS WITH A SINGLE STEP

In this activity you examine major stressors (events) in your life right now, previous major life events, and the daily hassles you experience as well as what pushes your buttons (i.e., triggers your anger).

A Journey Begins With a Single Step

Your journey of learning more about stress and stress management begins with paying attention to how stressful events manifest in you—in your body, emotions, and thoughts.

Stressful event	How does it feel in my body?	How do I feel emotionally?	What thoughts are associated with this event?

From N. Tummers, 2013, Stress Management: A Wellness Approach (Champaign, IL: Human Kinetics).

The Journey Begins With a Single Step worksheet is available in the appendix.

LIFESTYLE AND REDUCING STRESS

Review your lifestyle practices (behaviors you do most of the time) concerning finances, time management, alcohol and tobacco consumption, sexual practices, physical activity, anger management, and sleep. Reflect on which areas are most significantly tied to your experience of stress and where you may need to investigate ways to manage the stress caused by these practices.

CULTURAL EXPLORATION OF STRESS AND STRESS MANAGEMENT

This activity asks you to critically look at how our culture and society portray stressful situations and stress management. As we examine these portrayals, we can look at how our environment influences our own responses to stress.

- Select a movie you have watched recently. Consider how the characters view stressful situations and manage stress. How do you think you would behave if you were in a similar situation? Suggested movies: *Crash, Basketball Diaries, Six Degrees of Separation, Slumdog Millionaire, Stand and Deliver, The Blind Side, Secrets & Lies*.
- How do characters from different cultures and socioeconomic backgrounds experience and manage stress?
- How do your own social network and cultural identity affect how you respond to and manage stress? For example, if your social network revolves around being a student-athlete, do you experience stress as a result of pressure from coaches, your team, and the campus community?

AWARENESS OF STRESS AND STRESS MANAGEMENT

- What situations cause you to feel the most stressed?
- In what situations and activities do you feel the most relaxed?
- When you feel stressed, how do you normally react—both physically and emotionally?
- Based on your understanding of PNI, how does stress contribute to your health or risk of illness?

SIGNIFICANT LIFE CHANGES

- Reflect on significant changes you have experienced in your life. Make sure to review all the dimensions of wellness (physical, emotional, intellectual, social, spiritual, and environmental).
- When you reflected on your life changes, did you perceive them to be stressful or challenging?

- Reflect on the serenity prayer and your own life changes. Did you have an external or an internal locus of control during these events?
- Reflect on the importance of accepting that change is a process and of taking the time to be present and enjoy the journey.

THINGS THAT MAKE ME FLOW

List things you do that bring about a state of flow (loss of a sense of time and judgment while performing a challenging task that you have the skills to perform). Could you augment a sense of flow in your life?

CULTIVATING HARDINESS

Reflect on each of the qualities of hardiness: commitment, control, and challenge. When have you demonstrated these qualities? When have you observed these qualities in others? What were the specific situations? How could you cultivate these qualities more in your daily life?

PORTFOLIO OF STRENGTHS

Portfolio Activity

Set a goal to keep either a hard-copy or electronic portfolio in which you focus on strengths-based qualities you wish to cultivate, such as love, flow, and social support.

Portfolio artifacts can include a blog, a scrapbook, photos, a journal, poetry, short essays, letters, famous quotes, inspiring words, research studies, artwork, and playlists.

Summary

This chapter provided an overview of the science behind stress. Understanding how stress affects the body and its role in illness and disease is the first step to taking responsibility for your own stress management. In addition, this chapter presented the best in current scientific research regarding the best approach to stress management. A strengths-based approach focuses on proactive practices we can do daily to enhance our health and well-being.

The following chapters address each of the dimensions of wellness and provide activities to help you apply this information to your life in health-enhancing ways. We begin, in chapter 2, with the physical dimension of wellness and stress management.

chapter 2

Physical Wellness

He lives most life whoever breathes most air.

Elizabeth Barrett Browning

this chapter provides information, tools, and resources to help you set healthy lifestyle goals related to physical wellness and stress management. *Lifestyle* in this context refers to activities you practice consistently—every day or as often as possible. Such activities then become habits. You may already be practicing some of the physical wellness stress management tools, such as regular physical activity. In this chapter you will learn many simple ways to manage the physical dimension of wellness.

Many of the activities in this chapter start with mindful sitting. Here are some pointers to help you establish a mindful sitting practice:

- Sit up as tall and strong as possible in a comfortable chair. Loosen any restrictive clothing.
- Choose a quiet environment in which to practice. Turn off the phone.
- Focus on your breath. Find an anchor—a specific area such as your nostrils or the bridge of your nose—to keep bringing your full attention to as your breath enters and leaves your body.
- Be patient!

Acupuncture and Acupressure

Acupuncture and acupressure are used in traditional Chinese medicine and other Asian health modalities. Acupuncture uses fine-gauge needles (about the diameter of a cat's whisker), and acupressure uses steady pressure or tapping with the fingers to release stuck or blocked energy, or *chi*. The purpose of both methodologies is to decrease pain and increase energy.

@ WEB LINKS

Lifestyle and Physical Health

- Preventive Medicine Research Institute. This nonprofit institute provides research investigating the effects of lifestyle choices on health and disease. www.pmri.org
- RealAge. This website offers a test to determine an approximation of your real age (as opposed to your biological age) based on answers regarding lifestyle habits. Included are videos on living healthier lifestyles. Click on Daily Hassles to see how they "age" us. www.realage.com/mood-stress/are-daily-hassles-making-you-sick

Acupuncture

The National Certification Commission for Acupuncture and Oriental Medicine. This organization is a resource for finding reputable, state-licensed acupuncturists. www.nccaom.org

The National Institute of Neurological Disorders and Stroke estimates that about 45 million Americans suffer from chronic headaches. The most common form of headache is the tension headaches caused by constricted muscles in the head, neck, or scalp. Linde and colleagues (2009) reviewed 11 randomized trials of acupuncture on tension headaches in a total of 2,317 participants. They concluded that acupuncture is an effective treatment for frequent tension headaches.

TAPPING INTO POSITIVE ENERGY

In this activity you tap gently with your fingertips to release tension. The tapping is done with the three middle fingers with the same amount of firmness you would use when drumming your fingers on a desk. Use slow and soft movements for 30 to 60 seconds in each area.

START

Mindful sitting

CUES

1. Take a few deep, relaxing breaths. Bring both hands to your forehead. Begin tapping the space between your eyes for 30 to 60 seconds. Take five deep, relaxing breaths.
2. Bring both hands to the start of your eyebrows and tap while moving slowly outward until you've reached your temples. Take five deep, relaxing breaths.
3. Tap from above your ear, continuing behind your ear until you've reached the base of your skull where your neck begins. Continue with slow tapping.
4. Bring one arm across your body and tap the opposite wrist, elbow, shoulder joint, and top of the shoulder into the neck.
5. Take five deep breaths and switch sides.
6. With both hands, tap at the top of your sternum and slowly tap along your collarbone to the shoulder joint and back to the sternum. Take five relaxing breaths.

FINISH

Take five more relaxing breaths and notice how you feel after doing this acupressure tapping activity.

Autogenics

Autogenics is a self-administered tool that combats the fight or flight response. It consists of repeating phrases silently to oneself that encourage warmth as well as heaviness and relaxation in the extremities and then the whole body. *Autogenics* literally means "self-generating" (relaxation). It calms the body through vasodilation, an increase in the diameter of the blood vessels in response to parasympathetic nervous system activation. The result is reduced heart rate, blood pressure, breathing rate, and muscle tension. Autogenics is an effective way to deal with insomnia, headaches, and anxiety.

This tool might appeal to those who want to explore their kinesthetic intelligence and use a physically focused practice. At first, you will silently repeat the statements to yourself. As you become more proficient, you may find that you can achieve a state of relaxation without having to repeat the phrases. Be patient with this exercise and try not to force it—adopt an attitude of just trying it out.

THE BASICS OF AUTOGENICS

This activity will introduce the basics of practicing autogenics.

START

Mindful sitting or lying down

CUES

1. Close your eyes and come into a state of relaxed breathing.
2. Make a sincere effort to let go of any hassles or concerns from your day. Focus on bringing heaviness to your arms by repeating the following statements silently and slowly to yourself:
   - *My right arm is heavy.* (repeat three times)
   - *My left arm is heavy.* (repeat three times)
3. Feel the heaviness in your right arm. Feel the heaviness in your left arm.
4. Now repeat to yourself, *My right leg is heavy* three times and then, *My left leg is heavy* three times.
5. Feel the heaviness in your right leg. Feel the heaviness in your left leg.
6. Focus on your deep and relaxed breathing before proceeding.
7. Make a sincere effort once again to let go of distracting thoughts and focus on bringing warmth to your arms and legs by repeating the following statements slowly to yourself:
   - *My right arm and leg are warm.* (repeat three times)
   - *My left arm and leg are warm.* (repeat three times)
8. Feel the warmth in your right arm and leg. Feel the warmth in your left arm and leg.
9. Focus on your deep and relaxed breathing before proceeding.
10. Repeat the following statements:
    - *My whole body is warm and heavy.* (repeat three times)
    - *My heart rate is slow and calm.* (repeat three times)
    - *My breath is slow, deep, and relaxed.* (repeat three times)
    - *My forehead is cool.* (repeat three times)

FINISH

Rest quietly, enjoying the sensations of warmth and heaviness—the total relaxation you have created in your body and mind. Slowly open your eyes and take a moment to become aware of the room by gently stretching and taking some full, deep breaths. You should feel awake and refreshed.

QUICK AUTOGENICS WITH FOCUS ON BREATH

This quick form of autogenics can be done anywhere anytime you need a quick break to relax and become calm.

START

Mindful sitting

CUES

1. As you inhale, say quietly to yourself, *My breath is warm and calm.*
2. As you exhale, say quietly to yourself, *As I let the breath go, I let it wash away all my cares and worries.*
3. Repeat these statements as you inhale and exhale several more times until you feel relaxed and calm.

FINISH

Take a few more breaths and notice how you feel right now before starting your next activity.

USING IMAGINATION TO AUGMENT AUTOGENICS

This activity uses creative imagination to enhance the feelings of warmth and heaviness in your hands and fingers. See chapter 4 for more creative imagination activities.

START

Mindful sitting

CUES

1. Take a few deep, relaxing, centering breaths.
2. Sit upright with your hands resting comfortably on your thighs or on a table in front of you, with your palms up and fingers gently curled.
3. Imagine that you are sitting outside on a sunny day or at a sunny window. Imagine rays of sunshine covering your hands with warmth.
4. Feel your hands getting warmer and warmer.
5. Repeat silently to yourself as you imagine the sun's rays warming up your hands and arms: *My hands are warm and heavy.* Repeat this statement.
6. Feel your hands getting heavier and more relaxed with your next three deep and relaxed breaths.
7. Imagine the bones, ligaments, and tendons of the palms of your hands and all your fingers becoming softer with this warmth.
8. Imagine that you are holding a warm object such as a baked potato or a boiled egg. Permit your hands to become even warmer and heavier with your fingers slightly curled and relaxed as they lightly hold this warm object. Repeat once more to yourself: *My hands are warm and heavy.*

FINISH

Take a few more relaxed breaths and notice how you feel. Are there situations in which you might be able to use this activity, such as before a test or before writing a paper?

Biofeedback

Biofeedback is the process of attaining awareness and information (feedback) on physiological (bio) processes including body temperature, brain wave activity, heart rate, and blood pressure. Using various stress management techniques, these physiological processes can be modified to achieve healthy outcomes. At biofeedback clinics, trained clinicians use equipment to help patients gain awareness and practice modifying their responses to stress. However, sessions at such clinics can be costly.

Following are simple tools you can use to monitor your physiological variables. You can use stress management techniques to try to alter these variables.

- *Heart rate monitor.* People other than athletes can use this tool to measure heart rate. If you don't have a monitor, you can take a simple one-minute count of your heart rate and track it over time.

- *Blood pressure cuff.* You may know someone who has a blood pressure cuff and is willing to measure your blood pressure and help you track it over time. If not, use an automatic cuff available at a drugstore, or visit your school's health services.

- *Biodots.* These commercially available skin thermometers are placed on the hand and change color as blood flow to the extremities increases and decreases. Biodots are popular with students, who appreciate seeing the color change as they become calm and relaxed.

Breathing

Each of us has a distinct breathing pattern. Breathing is the most fundamental element of stress management, and how we breathe drastically affects our physiology and psychology. When we slouch or take short, inefficient, shallow breaths when upset, less oxygen is available to the body. This sets up a chain reaction of stress reactivity that includes elevated blood pressure and heart rate as the body senses it is not getting enough oxygen and nutrients. Our breath reflects our lives: when we keep a calm and relaxed focus, all the rest is background noise and we can choose to pay attention to it or not.

You may notice that babies sleeping peacefully breathe from their bellies. This is the natural breath pattern. The normal rate of breathing is about 12 to 15 breaths per minute. Slowing down your rate of breathing is one of the most effective stress management tools.

Breathing from the lower abdominal area engages a muscle called the *diaphragm*. This muscle separates the heart and lung cavity from the digestive cavity and other

@ WEB LINKS

Biofeedback

- Biofeedback Certification International Alliance. At this website you can search for certified biofeedback clinicians. www.bcia.org/i4a/pages/index.cfm?pageid=1

- Biodot Skin Thermometers. This commercially available tool provides biofeedback through the use of small dots placed on the skin. The color of the dot changes as you become relaxed or more stressed. www.biodots.net

organs. When the abdominal area fills up with air, the diaphragm drops allowing the lung cavity to enlarge and fill with more oxygen. The most relaxing part of the breath is the exhale, or out-breath. If you can place your attention on slowing down, lengthening, and calming your exhalation, you will be using one of the most effective stress management tools. By breathing correctly, the body becomes energized during inhalations and gets rid of impurities during exhalations. Through mindful, conscious, relaxed breathing, you can improve your blood pressure, heart rate, immune system, brain waves, digestion, and even sleep patterns.

You can practice your breathing stress management tools

- when waiting at a traffic light,
- before a test,
- before an athletic event,
- when frustrated or impatient, and
- before starting a difficult task.

Here are some tips for making the most of the breathing activities in this chapter:

- Practice makes perfect. Breathing may seem to be a natural skill, but many of us have unlearned how to breathe for health—we take shallow breaths and slump in our posture.
- If any cue or suggestion in this book is uncomfortable, modify it to meet your needs. This is your practice.
- Never force your breath. Allow it to be as easy and relaxed as possible. With practice, it will lengthen and deepen.
- Set a timer. Start with five minutes and slowly add more time.

Sitting up straight will allow you to take deeper breaths than if you slump and slouch. Try it. It will make you feel better!

TAKE TEN

When asked the magic number of breaths it takes for them to become calm and centered, many students say "Ten."

START

Mindful sitting

CUES

1. Seal your mouth lightly and close your eyes.
2. Come into relaxed breathing—breathing deeply into your belly.
3. On your next inhale, picture in your mind's eye, and say to yourself, the number 1 while gently inhaling as deeply as possible.
4. As you exhale, focus on, and say to yourself again, the number 1.
5. On the next inhale and exhale, focus on the number 2.
6. Repeat visualizing and quietly saying numbers until you reach 10.
7. If you notice you have become distracted, take a deep breath and start at 1 again.
8. Try not to make reaching the number 10 a task; rather, with each breath, feel focused and relaxed.

FINISH

Slowly come back to the room you are sitting in. Gently wiggle your fingers and toes. Stretch and take time to notice how you feel after completing this exercise.

LETTING-GO BREATH

This activity helps to move the focus of the breath from the upper lungs, where it is shallow and can cause more stress symptoms due to lack of oxygen, to the lower belly area. When breathing this way, we use the diaphragm muscle. This action stimulates the vagal nerve to bring about parasympathetic nervous system activation allowing us to rest and digest food, helping us to repair and replenish our essential bodily functions such as manufacturing immune cells.

START

Mindful sitting

CUES

1. Take some diaphragmatic breaths: breathe into the lower belly, then the ribs, and then the heart space. Take three more deep diaphragmatic breaths—comfortably deep and slow.
2. Bring your focus to the exhale, and on your next out-breath, perform a "letting-go breath"—sigh, let your body sink deeper into the chair or floor beneath you, and release all the muscles around your shoulders and neck. Let all tension, concerns, and whatever is on your mind just flow out as you make a sincere effort to just let go.
3. Try several more letting-go breaths on your own.

FINISH

When you are ready, bring your awareness back to the outside world, but at the same time hold on to the feeling of relaxation and calm that you created by letting go. Are there situations in your life in which you could use the letting-go breath?

OPEN THE THROAT

When we feel anxious, our throats become constricted; this can be exacerbated by poor posture. Additionally, a great deal of stress is held in the neck, shoulder, and throat area. This activity helps you release this tension.

START

This activity can be done seated or standing with a tall spine.

CUES

1. Move your neck, throat, and head area gently to help you relax. Try several shoulder shrugs and circles.

2. Slowly drop your chin into your chest and trace half-moons on your chest with your chin. Slowly bring your head back to neutral.

3. Slowly look over your right shoulders, take a deep breath, and hold this position. On your next exhale, let go of any tension in your right shoulder and neck area. Now gently dip your chin into your chest. Exhale deeply.

4. Slowly look over your left shoulder and hold this position. On your next exhale, let go of any tension in your right shoulder and neck area. Now gently dip your chin into your chest. Exhale deeply. Return your head to neutral.

5. Come back to your original position (sitting or standing). Make slow circles with your nose as if writing big, slow ovals on a chalkboard in front of your face; keep your head in front of your shoulders, not extended back.

6. Bring your shoulders up to your ears and release them again while making the sound "Ha." Do this two more times.

7. On the next inhale, yawn, taking in a big breath. Notice how it feels to have a relaxed and open throat area. On the exhale, softly say the sound "Ha." Experiment with saying "Ha" with your head back, your neck long, your chin tucked in toward your chest, and your head centered over your shoulders. Which positions result in a relaxed and open throat?

FINISH

Take a few more relaxing exhales letting the "Ha" sound like a deep, contented sigh as it floats out of your throat—calm and relaxed.

USING MANTRAS WITH THE BREATH

A mantra is a short, positive statement that can help focus your attention on your breath. In this activity, try to lengthen your exhalation, which is the most relaxing part of the breath.

START

Mindful sitting

CUES

Say quietly to yourself the following mantras.

1. On inhale: *Breathing in, I know that I'm breathing in.*
2. On exhale: *Breathing out, I know that I'm breathing out.*
3. On inhale: *Breathing in, I calm myself.*
4. On exhale: *Breathing out, I smile.*
5. On inhale: *Breathing in, I know that this is a perfect moment.*
6. On exhale: *Breathing out, I know that this is the only moment.*
7. On inhale: *I feel tension in my _____.*
8. On exhale: *I let go of that tension.*
9. On inhale: *I am here.*
10. On exhale: *Letting go.*

Notice whether specific words or phrases resonate with you and help you to maintain relaxed breathing. Use them as your own personal mantras as you continue to practice mantra breath.

FINISH

Come back to the space you are in, and take a few deep breaths before moving on to your next activity.

WHOLE BODY BREATHING

In this activity the whole body, not just the lungs, is engaged in relaxing breathing.

START

Mindful sitting

CUES

1. Feel your feet planted on the ground or floor. Imagine that they are soaking in warm air as you breathe in, and feel this warm air swirl upward around your ankles, shins, and kneecaps. Rest here, take another big inhale, and gently sigh out a big exhale.
2. On your next inhale, feel the intake of warm air swirling all the way up to your knees. Now pull the air up through your upper legs and hips. Feel the air continue to move up through your belly and chest and into your back body filling your entire core. Take a deep exhale.
3. Take a deep, relaxing inhale followed by an exhale and rest. On your next inhale, imagine warm air entering through your fingertips and up your arms,

surrounding your neck and shoulders with warm air. Feel the light, soothing, warm air saturate your skull and brain and face.

4. Imagine warm air filling your whole body.

FINISH

Take a deep breath and slowly return to the room you are in. Slowly stretch and yawn to open your body. Enjoy the relaxation you have created in your mind and body.

TAKE THREE MINUTES

This activity allows for a three-minute break to focus on and acknowledge what is going on but also to give you time to just breathe.

START

Mindful sitting

CUES

1. Minute 1: Bring an awareness to and acknowledge what is going on. What is on your mind? How does your body feel? How are you feeling emotionally?
2. Minute 2: Shift your attention to your breath and keep your focus there.
3. Minute 3: Let your whole body breathe in a relaxed and calm manner.

FINISH

At the end of your three-minute break, come back to the room and your next activity with renewed vitality and focus.

WAKE-UP BREATH

This breathing activity is a good one for becoming awake and energized. This pose helps you practice what it feels like to use your diaphragm muscle.

START

Mindful sitting

CUES

1. With your mouth sealed, take a full, deep intake of air through your nostrils.
2. On the exhale, release the air through your nose with quick, short bursts of air. Emphasize contracting your diaphragm by drawing your belly button quickly in toward your spine. See if you can do three or four blasts of exhaled air before you need to take another inhale.
3. Take a deep, full inhale through your nostrils.
4. On the exhale, fold forward resting your upper body on your thighs while exhaling all the air in your lungs through an open mouth, drawing your belly button to your spine.
5. Slowly sit up and take a few relaxing breaths.
6. Continue the cycle, working toward getting 8 to 10 short bursts on the exhale followed by the deep inhale and full exhale while folding forward.

FINISH

Rest for a few moments in seated child pose (folding at the hips and resting the upper body on your thighs, arms hanging loosely at your sides or resting on your knees or shins).

TRIANGLE BREATH

In this activity you use the image of a triangle to visualize your breath being largest at the base of the triangle, which is superimposed over your torso.

START

Mindful sitting

CUES

1. Imagine a large triangle superimposed over the trunk of your body.
2. The base of the triangle covers the "seat belt" muscle. imagine breathing deeply into the base of the triangle filling in both the front and back of your lower trunk.
3. Allow your breath to slowly fill in the sides of the triangle until you reach the top of the triangle, situated at your throat.
4. Slowly let out the exhale, first from your heart, then your ribs. By drawing your belly button to your spine, let the air out of your lower belly as slowly as is comfortable.
5. Continue practicing triangle breath.

FINISH

Rest comfortably for a few moments enjoying the effects of using this relaxed breathing technique.

ALTERNATE NOSTRIL BREATHING

This activity is said to access both hemispheres of the brain. After practicing and getting into the rhythm of this breath, many students find this activity their favorite one to do before a difficult task such as a homework assignment or test. It takes a few cycles to get into the rhythm of this breath exercise, but you will find yourself more awake and energized as you get used to it.

START

Mindful sitting

CUES

1. Use the thumb and index finger (or middle finger) of your right hand to lightly close off each nostril as you slowly inhale and exhale through the other nostril.
2. Slowly inhale through your right nostril and lightly pinch off, or close, your left nostril with your index finger.
3. Slowly release the left nostril and exhale through the left nostril while pinching, or closing off, the right nostril with your thumb.

4. Inhale through the left nostril (the right nostril is still pinched off) and then release the right nostril and exhale slowly through the right nostril as the left nostril is closed off by the index finger.

5. Repeat the cycles several times to get the hang of alternating the breath in and out of individual nostrils.

VARIATION

In this variation you use your mind to imagine blocking off each nostril instead of physically doing it. It takes some patience to get the hang of it, but it can be done readily in a classroom or public space without anyone knowing what you are doing!

FINISH

Take a few natural breaths as you continue to sit quietly, and notice how you feel after practicing alternate nostril breathing.

Healthy Eating

Stress rules when it comes to our eating habits; it affects how much we eat, when we eat, and what we want to eat. This may be a foreign concept, but the body and brain want only one thing: fuel so they can work. Stress also strongly affects our nutritional status: the ability to digest and absorb nutrients and eliminate toxins and waste. Under stress, digestion slows down and elimination can be disrupted (e.g., diarrhea or irritable bowel syndrome). When we are rushed and not paying attention to what we are eating, we are likely to overeat as well as not to chew our food well enough for optimal digestion.

The gastrointestinal tract contains a significant quantity of neurons and neurotransmitters, such as serotonin, so much so that it has been termed "the second brain" (Gershon, 1998). The traditional Hindu system of medicine called ayurvedic medicine focuses on nutrition and digestion (National Center for Complementary and Alternative Medicine, 2009). Meanwhile, most medical students in the United States receive minimal nutrition education within their required curriculums (Adams, Kohlmeier, & Zeisel, 2010). In addition, a staggering number of commercials assert that poor nutrition and digestion problems are part of the normal human experience. These messages may reinforce the notion that overeating is a cultural norm.

Foods that can actually cause stress reactivity have been called "pseudo stressors" (Greenberg, 2008, p. 84). We often crave foods that stimulate our bodies to go into the fight or flight response; the culprits rampant at most colleges are processed foods, sugar, alcohol, and caffeine. As these foods are consumed, the body feels better because of an increase in blood sugar and serotonin levels. However, as these levels rise, the body reacts with stress symptoms such as increased heart rate and blood pressure. When blood sugar levels start to drop, the body may crave anything that will increase the buzz or energy level, starting a roller coaster of seeking out more substances that improve mood and energy levels—the "pseudo stressors." This makes things worse by also increasing stress reactivity, stress hormones, blood pressure, and heart rate, putting the body into a constant state of allostatic load.

Caffeine

Caffeine is a substance naturally found in coffee and chocolate and added to many products such as soft drinks and pain relievers. It is a drug that stimulates the sympathetic nervous system by increasing heart rate and blood pressure. According to James Lane, an expert in caffeine research at Duke University, the repeated increases in blood pressure and stress reactivity caused by caffeine could contribute to an increased risk of coronary heart disease in adults (Lane et al., 2002). In addition, caffeine causes the adrenal glands to kick out epinephrine, which triggers the liver to release stored sugars into the bloodstream; in turn, the pancreas must release insulin to balance the rising blood sugar levels. According to Lane's extensive research, caffeine upsets glucose metabolism and could contribute to developing impaired glucose tolerance. The elevated amounts of glucose caused by caffeine intake can also cause mood swings as the body adjusts to increased and then plummeting levels of glucose. As the effects wear off, the roller coaster of ups and downs in mood, energy, and concentration levels starts again.

Refined Sugar

One of the most important nutrients is carbohydrate. This substance provides energy so cells can work. Carbohydrate is digested, and the resulting sugar, known as glucose, is absorbed into the bloodstream and used by the cells. How quickly the sugar is available depends on the kind of carbohydrate eaten. *Complex carbohydrate*, which has had minimal processing and is still in a complex chemical state such as a vegetable, takes longer for the body to break down into glucose than simple carbohydrate. This results in a slower, more even release of glucose into the bloodstream. This slower release of glucose can be further prolonged if the complex carbohydrate is also high in fiber (e.g., 100 percent whole grain bread) or eaten with fat or protein. Processed, or refined, sugar is processed before consumption. Examples of simple carbohydrates are white sugar refined from sugar cane and high fructose corn syrup refined from corn.

According to Marion Nestle (Paulette Goddard Professor in the Department of Nutrition, Food Studies, and Public Health and Professor of Sociology at New York University), refined sugar is in most processed foods, especially soft drinks. These refined sugars are quickly absorbed into the bloodstream with resulting rapid increases in blood sugar levels. Trying to maintain allostasis, or balance, the body reacts by releasing insulin to help glucose exit the bloodstream and enter cells.

@ WEB LINKS

Caffeine

- Center for Science in the Public Interest (CSPI). This nonprofit organization is a valuable resource for nonbiased nutrition information. Its twin missions are "to conduct research and advocacy programs in health and nutrition, and to provide consumers with current, useful information about their health and well-being." www.cspinet.org/about/index.html
- CSPI caffeine chart. Energy bars, energy drinks, chocolate, and even some forms of headache medications contain caffeine. You can check the CSPI caffeine chart for the caffeine content of food, beverages, and drugs. www.cspinet.org/new/cafchart.htm

Nutrition

Marion Nestle is an outstanding resource on nutrition and the politics involved in how and what we eat. www.foodpolitics.com/about

The high levels of blood sugar then drop quickly as the body strives for allostasis resulting in hypoglycemia, or lowered blood sugar. The side effects often seen with hypoglycemia are crankiness, anxiety, and headaches.

When we eat highly processed sugars while also experiencing a stressful situation (e.g., driving and eating), the release of stress hormones such as cortisol can interfere with digestion and cause further allostatic load. When stress is unrelenting, cortisol can inhibit the body's ability to produce adequate amounts of insulin. The body consequently becomes insulin resistant, experiences abnormal blood sugar levels, and can eventually develop diabetes. The bottom line is that eating highly processed foods keeps your body from getting the nutrition it needs to keep you healthy and fight off illness.

Refined sugar goes by many names, including high fructose corn syrup, sucrose, lactose, dextrose, honey, invert sugar, malt syrup, maple syrup, maltose, raw sugar, molasses, beet sugar, sugar, turbinado sugar, brown sugar, and corn syrup. Check food labels for these.

Alcohol

When we use the term *alcohol*, we are referring to ethanol, an organic substance made by fermenting and distilling products containing glucose such as corn, grapes, and grains. When the glucose product is refined, it becomes very dense with calories. In fact, alcohol has almost as many calories per grams as fat (7 calories per gram versus 9 calories per gram for fat). It is easy to consume a large amount of these calories in a short period of time. Another problem is that alcoholic drinks are often mixed with refined sugars; the two substances combined can really stress the body with excess weight. Alcoholic drinks with sugar stress both the liver (to metabolize the alcohol) and the pancreas (to deal with excess blood sugar).

The following list outlines side effects of alcohol intake (American College Health Association, 2011):

- Physical symptoms: Nausea, dehydration, sleep disruption, stomach upset, headache
- Behavior: Arguments, poor judgment, lack of motivation, poor academic performance, absenteeism, inability to concentrate on studying or in class

The following list contains some facts about alcohol (U.S. Centers for Disease Control and Prevention, 2012):

- The age group with the most binge drinkers is 18- to 34-year-olds.
- Most alcohol-impaired drivers binge drink.
- Most people who binge drink are not alcohol dependent or alcoholics.
- More than half of the alcohol adults drink is while binge drinking.
- More than 90 percent of the alcohol youth drink is while binge drinking.

Many students find that alcohol helps them to relax or take the edge off. The pharmacological action, or drug effect, of alcohol on the body is as a depressant. How alcohol affects each individual depends on numerous factors. A study published in *Alcoholism: Clinical and Experimental Research* (Childs, O'Connor, & de Wit, 2011) revealed that, although alcohol can decrease the hormonal response to stress, at the same time it can also extend the negative subjective experience of the stressor. Stress was also shown to decrease the enjoyable effects of drinking. Childs and colleagues stated that these findings demonstrate complicated "bi-directional" interactions between stress and alcohol that could lead to drinking more alcohol, alcohol dependency, or both.

Because alcohol is a depressant, students can react to its effects with depression, anxiety, suicidal thoughts, poor decisions such as risky sexual behaviors, or violence, or become prone to unintentional and intentional injuries. Alcohol is of concern as a stressor because it reduces brain activity as a result of the decreased activity of neurotransmitters. However, excessive use such as binging has its own associated set of stressors: grades go down as the number of drinks per week increases; violence and sexual assault incidents rise; and people experience increased risk of other health issues such as STIs and unwanted pregnancies.

Following are tips for reducing the risk of alcohol abuse:

- Avoid pregaming (excessive drinking at home before going out to a club or event). Avoid places that push drinking, such as keggers, casinos, or "women drink free" night at clubs and bars.

- Be aware of how much you drink and under what circumstances—know your personal limit.

- Commit to using other stress management tools when you feel the urge to drink as a coping mechanism, such a physical activity or taking a walk with a good listener.

- Respect others' right not to drink; stand up for your own choice not to drink.

- Bring less money to a bar and commit to not borrowing money or using your ATM card.

- Make sure to eat and hydrate when consuming alcohol.

- Pace yourself; switch off between alcoholic drinks and water or other non-alcoholic beverages.

- Bring your own cup to a party. You don't need to advertise what you are drinking, but you will have a drink to hold on to.

- Be aware of combining alcohol and energy drinks or other drugs including over-the-counter medications and prescriptions.

- Commit with your friends to using a designated driver, and make sure to take your turn. The designated driver does not drink at all.

- If someone who has been drinking becomes unresponsive, you need to take action. Do not delay hoping the person will shake it off; call 911.

- Consider other ways to socialize and bond with your friends that do not include alcohol. For example, some schools have established "alternative spring breaks" where students volunteer to do a service project with their classmates instead of going to a destination to get wasted.

Hydration and Dehydration

Hydration and dehydration also affect our health. According to a report compiled by a panel of specialists in the area of water consumption (Institute of Medicine, 2005): "Dehydration or body water deficits challenge the ability of the body to maintain homeostasis during perturbations (e.g., sickness, physical exercise, or climatic stress) and can impact function and health" (p. 4). Dehydration can lead to headaches, dizziness, and confusion. Adequate hydration helps the body function optimally, although what constitutes adequate hydration varies among individuals. One way to know whether you are adequately hydrated is to evaluate your urine. It should be the color of pale lemonade. Check out the urine color chart at www.navyfitness.org/nutrition/noffs_fueling_series/hydrate/.

Core Alcohol and Drug Survey Statistics

The Core Alcohol and Drug Survey is the largest survey conducted to measure alcohol and other drug usage, attitudes, and perceptions among college students at two- and four-year institutions. The following are some key findings on the use of alcohol:

- 81.7 percent of students consumed alcohol in the past year.
- 68.3 percent of students consumed alcohol in the past 30 days.
- 62.4 percent of underage students (younger than 21) consumed alcohol in the previous 30 days.
- 43.1 percent of students reported binge drinking in the previous two weeks. A binge is defined as consuming five or more drinks in one sitting.

The following are some key findings on the use of illegal drugs:

- 30.2 percent of students have used marijuana in the past year.
- 17.2 percent of students are current marijuana users.

The following are reported consequences that occurred at least once during the past year as a result of drinking or drug use:

- 34.8 percent reported some form of public misconduct (such as trouble with police, fighting, DUI, and vandalism).
- 22.7 percent reported experiencing some kind of serious personal problems such as thoughts or attempts at suicide, being hurt or injured, trying unsuccessfully to stop using, and sexual assault.

Reprinted, by permission, from the Core Institute, 2009, *Core Institute Core Alcohol and Drug Survey Executive Summary Report* (Carbondale, IL: SIUC/Core Institute).

Following are actions you can take to make sure you are well hydrated:

- Drink fluids (water should be your first choice).
- Avoid beverages that contain excessive caffeine or are sources of excessive calories (or both), such as fluid replacement drinks and high-fat coffee drinks.
- If you are outdoors or engaging in physical activity, or both, in hot or humid conditions, don't let thirst be your barometer to hydrate. Drink consistently throughout the activity and the day.

When the body is dehydrated, it becomes stressed and reacts by going into the fight or flight response. Many of us misinterpret the stress signals and reach for food when our bodies actually need fluids.

Stress Eating

Stress eating is common among college students. When the body is experiencing stress reactivity, the primary concern is survival. It goes into emergency mode by releasing both glucose (known as blood sugar) and fat into the bloodstream to fuel the physical demands of fighting or fleeing. The brain functions only on the fuel source of glucose, or blood sugar. Cortisol works in association with other hormones to break down fat and carbohydrate to be used as extra energy sources. This initially decreases appetite and intensifies alertness, preparing the body for action. After the threat has diminished, cortisol performs its second function, which is to get the body back to balance, or allostasis. It does this by signaling an increase in appetite to replace the carbohydrate and fat that would have been burned while fleeing or fighting. The body assumes that a bout of physical exertion has just taken place (e.g., running from a predator) and that energy reserves must be restocked—even when that is not the case. This is how cortisol affects body weight.

According to Stanford University biologist Robert M. Sapolsky (2004), elevated levels of cortisol increase not only hunger and appetite, but also the production of glucose. When that glucose is then not used, it is stored as fat, increasing body weight. So the sad truth is, you are probably still sitting in your car or at your desk, still fuming and stressed out, and eating a lot of carbohydrates or fatty foods that your body doesn't need and therefore stores as body fat.

Chronic stress can result in an excessive release of cortisol and other hormones. If the stress reaction continues, the levels of hormones continue to demand and burn energy, causing the blood sugar level to drop. When this happens a phenomenon called food-seeking behavior, or grazing and gorging, occurs. The body seeks the best food choices for survival: high-fat and high-sugar foods. When we eat these foods, our bodies secrete serotonin, which makes us feel calm and stops the release of cortisol. If we continue to be stressed or haven't dealt with whatever is stressing us, the cycle starts all over again. Figure 2.1 depicts how this cycle is perpetuated.

Stock up on healthy snacks like fruits and vegetables so that you can provide your body with healthy vitamins and nutrients. Having healthy food readily available will help you to avoid compulsively consuming junk food if you find yourself stress eating.

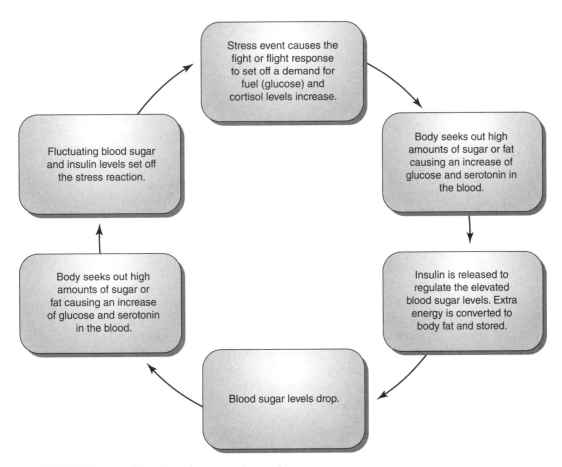

FIGURE 2.1   The stress/stress-eating cycle.

Here are some action steps you can take toward adopting a stress management diet.

- If you are a stress eater, plan ahead so that you do not become overwhelmed and reach for food. Here are some specific things you can do:
  - Bring healthy snacks to keep your blood sugar levels stable during a long day at school or work.
  - Take a break from a stressful task such as homework and go for a walk; do a favorite hobby such as playing the piano or a video game.
  - Leave unhealthy snack foods off your shopping list so they are not available; find healthy snacks that you enjoy. Read labels and be cognizant of portion sizes.
  - Engage in a relaxing activity such as listening to quiet music or doing some yoga poses.
  - Find a "stress buddy" to talk with when you are feeling overwhelmed, someone who will hold you accountable to your commitment not to engage in stress eating.
- If you tend to not eat when stressed, make sure to keep up your energy stores with healthy food choices like heart-healthy fats such as olive oil; high-quality

proteins such as lean meats, low- or no-fat dairy, beans, and legumes; and high-density carbohydrates such as green leafy vegetables and whole grains.

- Enjoy smaller, well-spaced meals and snacks (see the healthy eating plate in figure 2.2) that consist of quality protein, complex whole carbohydrates, and vegetable and fruits. Eat healthy snacks such as almonds.

- Dieting can also set off the stress response. The body reacts because it senses it is being threatened: starvation! Eating small, well-spaced, high-quality meals and snacks is a better choice than dieting. Dieting doesn't work in the long run, and the perpetual yo-yo of gaining and losing weight can be a significant stressor in itself. Set up a healthy eating plan that can be part of your lifestyle for the long haul. Allow for treats in moderation.

- Listen to your body. If you are craving something, can you have a small amount as a treat, not as a meal? Can you take a few bites and be satisfied?

- Don't listen to the craving; instead, find someone to confide in so you can reward or soothe yourself without food.

- Pay attention when you eat; eat mindfully. *Mindful eating* means just eating and not engaging in other distracting activities at the same time such as watching TV or driving. It is hard to pay attention to cues of fullness and satisfaction when distracted. Chapter 4 contains a mindful eating activity.

- Practice waiting. Ask yourself whether you are really hungry or whether you are letting the clock dictate when you should eat. Drink some water in case you are just dehydrated, and try to eat in response to hunger, not the clock.

- Keep tempting foods out of sight and out of mind. Ask roommates, partners, and family members not to bring junk food into the house. Think of junk food as an occasional treat. Go out for special treats with friends rather than eating a pint of ice cream mindlessly in front of the computer, so the experience is focused more on the social aspect.

- Eat high-quality low-fat or nonfat protein; you need protein to create hormones and enzymes as well as to build and repair cells.

Protein

Consuming too much protein can also strain the body because of its inability to store excess dietary protein. Such protein is converted to either glucose or stored glycogen or to body fat. Because the by-products of this process must be flushed out of the body, dehydration can result. How much protein do people need to consume? The answer varies from person to person. The general recommendation for women (ages 19 to 70) is 46 grams per day, and for men (ages 19 to 70), 56 grams per day (U.S. Centers for Disease Control and Prevention, 2011b). People who are pregnant, healing from surgery, or doing strenuous muscle activity such as weightlifting will need more protein.

Carbohydrate

Carbohydrates are essential nutrients that provide the energy necessary for cells to function. But not all carbohydrates are the same. The glycemic index (GI) is a scale from 1 to 100 based on how quickly specific foods cause blood glucose levels to rise. *Low-glycemic-index foods* are a good alternative to processed or high-sugar foods. Foods with a GI under 50, such as All Bran cereal (42) and black beans (30), take a while to digest and therefore result in a slower rise in blood sugar. These foods would be a better choice than those with a GI over 70, such as the high-sugar breakfast cereal Coco Pops (77) or a deep-fried doughnut (75). High-GI foods can have low GI ratings when eaten with low-fat protein choices such as eggs and chicken because these foods take longer to digest.

The habitual intake of high-glycemic-index foods can cause a chronic inflammation response (Bosma-den Boer, van Welten, & Priumboom, 2012), which increases allostatic load. On the other hand, if the body does not get enough carbohydrate, it will use protein either from the diet or from muscle to generate blood glucose. Remember, the brain and nervous system use glucose to perform their functions. However, when the body uses a noncarbohydrate source such as protein to generate glucose, this process (known as *gluconeogenesis*) puts a lot of strain on the body because it is an inefficient way to create glucose. The by-products of this process also stress the body. One of the harmful by-products is caused when the body has elevated ketone levels; as the kidneys filter out these harmful ketones, kidney stones can develop.

Vitamins and Minerals

Vitamins and minerals serve as catalysts that allow our bodies to utilize the other nutrients of carbohydrate, protein, fat, and water for biological functions. When under stress, the body cannot absorb calcium into the intestines. Other important minerals such as copper, magnesium, potassium, and zinc are not absorbed either. As a result, the body must use its own calcium stores (in bones) to perform the functions that require this mineral. This sets the body up for osteoporosis, weaknesses in the bone structure, and possibly fractures. So not only do we need to take in enough vitamins by eating a variety of healthy foods (especially fresh fruits and vegetables) every day, but also we need to manage stress to ensure that those vitamins are absorbed properly.

The following are some facts and tips about vitamins and minerals and the roles they play with stress.

@ WEB LINKS AND RESOURCE

Mindful Eating

- Center for Mindful Eating. This is a great resource for up-to-date research and information on mindful eating. www.tcme.org
- Albers, S. (2006). *Mindful eating 101: A guide to healthy eating in college and beyond*. New York: Routledge Taylor Francis Group.

Glycemic Index

These links will help you calculate the glycemic index of foods.

- Academy of Nutrition and Dietetics. This organization is a source of sound nutrition advice and resources. www.eatright.org
- Harvard Medical School. This site lists the glycemic index levels of over 100 foods. www.health.harvard.edu/newsweek/Glycemic_index_and_glycemic_load_for_100_foods.htm

Vitamins, Minerals, and Stress

- Vitamins have no calories and therefore provide no energy. Their function is to prevent disease, regulate bodily processes, and help the body use the major nutrients. When the body is under stress, it produces cortisol, a process that requires vitamins. Too much stress can cause the body to be depleted of vitamins such as B complex and C resulting in symptoms such as anxiety and depression.

- Minerals do not provide energy, either; their function is to regulate body functions and make up the structure of hard and soft tissues (e.g., bone). Consider green leafy vegetables, whole grains, beans, strawberries, and citrus fruits as great sources of minerals! Again, as with vitamins, the best way to make sure we get the best nutrition is not only to eat healthy foods but also to practice consistent stress management.

- The benefits of taking vitamin B complex, vitamin C, calcium, potassium, zinc, and magnesium can be lost when they are not absorbed as a result of stress reactivity or excessive urine output from, you guessed it, caffeine and alcohol!

- Dark chocolate (in moderation) contains phytochemicals that protect the cells from stress and inflammation. Phytochemicals lower levels of cortisol. David Katz, director of the Prevention Research Center at Yale University School of Medicine, recommends a moderate intake of dark chocolate—just over 2 ounces (57 g) per week, or a few small squares (Katz, Doughty, & Ali, 2011).

- Nuts and seeds contain omega-3 fatty acids, which improve mood, calm inflammation, and contain melatonin that maintains brain function. A serving of nuts or seeds is 0.5 ounce (15 g), or 1 tablespoon of peanut butter (U.S. Department of Agriculture, n.d.). Keep in mind that this is considered a 1-ounce (30 g) protein serving and that the recommended protein limit is 5 to 7 ounces (150 to 200 g) per day.

Balanced Nutrition

The U.S. government recently adopted a new nutrition information graphic called ChooseMyPlate (see figure 2.2) that you can use to develop a healthy eating plan. We can all make better food choices without labeling some foods as "bad." Eating foods considered bad can perpetuate feelings of being a bad person. Disordered eating habits can result when people become obsessed with foods they must eat or cannot eat. To have a healthy diet, we need to eat healthy foods to nourish ourselves, eat

@ WEB LINKS

Nutrition

- U.S. Department of Agriculture. ChooseMyPlate.gov. This website offers more information on daily nutritional needs. www.choosemyplate.gov/food-groups/downloads/TenTips/DGTipsheet6ProteinFoods.pdf

- National Institutes of Health DASH Eating Plan (Dietary Approaches to Stop Hypertension). Dietary Approach to Stop Hypertension (DASH) is a flexible eating plan that has been found to be successful in lowering blood pressure. www.nhlbi.nih.gov/health/public/heart/hbp/dash/new_dash.pdf

FIGURE 2.2   U.S. Department of Agriculture's ChooseMyPlate.
Reprinted from USDA's Center for Nutrition Policy and Promotion.

in moderation, and enjoy foods that help us to maintain optimal health. As much as possible, choose whole grains, healthy proteins, and fresh fruit and vegetables.

KEEPING A FOOD LOG

One of the most effective ways to bring awareness to your eating is to keep a food log. Most successful weight loss programs such as Weight Watchers use this method. Online apps can make this task easier as well.

START

Find a method to accurately record everything you eat and drink.

CUES

1. Keep a log of everything you eat and drink for a week (portions sizes are important!). Include the time you ate, how hungry you were, and how you were feeling (e.g., stressed or hurried and whether you ate mindfully).

2. Take a look at your week and circle any problems you see. Brainstorm ways to resolve these problems. For example, if you notice that you drink a lot of caffeine with sugar and always have a sweet pastry in the afternoon, can you think of a substitute such as taking a walk, trying an herbal drink, or eating a half portion?

3. Take the healthy eating challenge. The ideas that follow can help to jump start your actions toward healthy eating. Think of them as experiments to increase your awareness, and then consider taking small steps toward healthier habits. The idea is to record a baseline of what you typically eat for a week. Then, take an honest look and set a challenge for the following two weeks and see how it goes. Use this experiment to pay attention to how you feel and how your stress levels are when you choose healthier alternatives.

    - Take a baseline of how much coffee or caffeine you drink by keeping a log for a week. Then set a challenge to reduce your coffee or caffeine consumption.

    - Take a baseline of your sugar consumption. This might involve recording all the food and beverages you consume for a week and then determining how much refined sugar you take in. Pay attention to store-bought cookies and muffins, soda, and sugar added to cereal or coffee. Become a detective to see where sugar might be hiding in your diet, and set a goal to reduce the amount by a specific number of servings.

- Keep a baseline of your beverage intake including juice, soda, and water. One area that may be of interest is alcohol consumption, but be aware that when we drink excessively, we often lose count.
- Snack switch-out week. After you have looked at your baseline for snacks, substitute a healthier alternative for a typical snack each day. For example, if you eat potato chips, switch to salsa with veggies and whole grain chips.

FINISH

As you continue to use the food diary, reflect on what healthy choices you have made and wish to continue. What are ways you can be successful at making small but significant changes in your daily nutrition?

Tobacco Use

College students smoke for a variety of reasons. Many smoke to manage stress. According to a study conducted by researchers at the Tobacco Etiology Research Network (Tiffany et al., 2007), college students typically take a break to smoke to take their minds off a stressful event, or they believe that smoking helps them deal with stressors. Smoking also has a powerful social context: it is seen as means of socializing as well as a way to empathize with another person who is stressed by sharing while smoking. Many students don't realize, however, that nicotine, a stimulant, actually causes stress reactivity by increasing blood pressure and heart rate and lowering the delivery of oxygen to the brain. The addictive aspects of nicotine

@ WEB LINKS

Healthy Eating

- Harvard School of Public Health. Healthy Eating Plate and Healthy Eating Pyramid. www.hsph.harvard.edu/nutritionsource/what-should-you-eat/pyramid
- Johns Hopkins School of Public Health. This prestigious institution has a link for research and centers that focus on various health topics including nutrition and mental health. www.jhsph.edu/research/centers-and-institutes/center-for-human-nutrition/
- International Foundation for Functional Gastrointestinal Disorders. This resource offers health information and research to help those with chronic GI disorders. www.iffgd.org

Smoking Cessation

- U.S. Centers for Disease Control and Prevention (CDC). The CDC offers smoking cessation resources. www.cdc.gov/tobacco/quit_smoking/how_to_quit/index.htm
- American Cancer Society. This website offers many resources to help people quit smoking. www.cancer.org

aren't surprising because of the release of acetylcholine, which increases attention span, and dopamine, which is associated with pleasure.

Many stress management techniques can counteract these addictive aspects and help you quit smoking. Consider meditation or exercise as substitutes when you need to take a break or refocus.

Recommendations for Quitting Tobacco Use

- Take the time to examine how your use of tobacco influences your overall health. Explore all the dimensions. Consider whether your habit influences the health of others (e.g., exposing roommates or younger siblings to side-stream smoke).

- Make a commitment to quit or to cut back on cigarettes. Recognize that quitting takes dedication and time. Give yourself time, taking it day by day, minute by minute.

- Find out your options. Seek help on your campus such as support groups. Find out about nicotine replacement products or cessation prescription medications.

- Make a commitment with a friend to find ways to socialize without lighting up.

Sexual Health

Two of the top life event stressors for college students are diagnoses of sexually transmitted infections (STIs, also sometimes referred to as *sexually transmitted diseases*, or *STDs*) and unwanted pregnancies. Safe practices and self-care regarding sexual health are firmly rooted in the healthy practices advocated in this text: managing emotions, communicating assertively, standing up for your rights, making responsible choices, having a strong supportive social network, and avoiding the excessive use of alcohol or other drugs. Education and communication are the most important tools for lowering the risk of unintended pregnancy, intimate partner violence, rape, and STIs.

Recommendations for Reducing Sexual Risk

- Practice good self-care including pregnancy prevention, or birth control, whether you are female or male. However, using birth control does not always protect against STIs. For example, the birth control pill does not prevent the transmittal of STIs.

- Educate yourself about current sexuality issues. Although knowledge is the best prevention tool, keep in mind that the only 100 percent effective form of STI and pregnancy prevention is abstinence.

- See your health care provider regularly, and be honest about your sexual history.

- Be aware of the symptoms of STIs, but also understand that many STIs can be asymptomatic (i.e., not showing any apparent or outward symptoms).

- Get tested. Take advantage of the screening and services provided by your campus health care center or local health care provider.

- Limit the number of sexual partners.

- Use male and female condoms or a cervical diaphragm as protective barriers in addition to birth control (e.g., the pill).

Remember: education and communication are the most important tools for preventing and lowering the risk for unintended pregnancy, intimate partner violence, rape, and STIs.

Rape and Intimate Partner Violence

Intimate partner violence (IPV) happens between two people in a close relationship. This relationship can be current or in the past and includes spouses and dating partners. The violence can be physical as well as emotional. It is important to realize that both males and females can be the subject of this violence. Please see the Web Links: Rape and Intimate Partner Violence sidebar for more information.

Massage Therapy and Therapeutic Touch

According to the American Massage Therapy Association, massage is a medically established stress management tool (www.amtamassage.org). The U.S. National

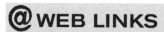

@ WEB LINKS

Sexual Health

Planned Parenthood. This organization is an important resource for responsible self-care regarding sexual health for both sexes. www.plannedparenthood.org

Rape and Intimate Partner Violence

- U.S. Centers for Disease Control and Prevention. VetoViolence (Violence Education Tools Online). This is a Facebook page about violence prevention. www.facebook.com/vetoviolence
- National Center on Domestic and Sexual Violence. This organization encourages collaboration among professionals working to end violence against women. www.ncdsv.org/ncd_about.html
- 911rape. This information website is provided by the Rape Treatment Center at UCLA Medical Center, Santa Monica. www.911rape.org/home
- The Clothesline Project. This project offers violence and rape victims the chance to artistically decorate a T-shirt to give them a nonconfrontational way to voice what happened to them. www.clotheslineproject. org/About_Shirts.htm

Massage Therapy and Therapeutic Touch

- National Center for Complementary and Alternative Medicine. This organization provides information on research and upcoming research trials in massage therapy. http://nccam.nih.gov/health/massage
- American Massage Therapy Association. This website can help you locate a licensed massage therapist (LMT) is your area. www.amtamassage. org/index.html
- Therapeutic Touch. This website provides research on and information about the use of therapeutic touch. www.therapeutictouch.org

Institutes of Health, however, has stated that conclusive research on how massage therapy works is limited. Nevertheless, a summary of current research suggests that after just one session of massage therapy, people experienced reductions in anxiety, blood pressure, and heart rate. Also, after multiple sessions of massage therapy, people were found to be less prone to general anxiety, depression, and pain.

Tiffany Fields heads the Touch Research Institute (TRI; n.d.) at the University of Miami's Miller School of Medicine. She researches both massage therapy and therapeutic touch (TT), a method in which a practitioner directs energy toward a patient's healing, usually without physical contact. Fields has conducted extensive research (over 100 studies) on the benefits of both massage and therapeutic touch on health outcomes. Following are some of her significant research findings: "enhanced growth (e.g., in preterm infants), diminished pain (e.g., fibromyalgia), decreased autoimmune problems (e.g., increased pulmonary function in asthma and decreased glucose levels in diabetes), enhanced immune function (e.g., increased natural killer cells in HIV and cancer), and enhanced alertness and performance (e.g., EEG pattern of alertness and better performance on math computations)." The researchers at TRI go on to state that "many of these effects appear to be mediated by decreased stress hormones" (Touch Research Institute, n.d.).

SELF-MASSAGE

This activity helps to bring awareness to stress held in the face and neck areas. Experiment with various massage movements including the following:

- Jostling or shaking to loosen up the area; smoothing or gliding over the area by brushing lightly
- Friction: rubbing in a circular movement with gentle pressure
- Kneading
- Tapping

START
Mindful sitting

CUES
1. Scrunch up your eyebrows and allow them to relax. Using your fingertips, gently smooth out your forehead area with light pressure. Gently tap this area and experiment with various massage movements all over your forehead.
2. Massage your jaw joints with light pressure from your fingers in small circles.
3. Massage your eye socket area with your index fingers. Starting at the top of your nose, slowly move down with gentle, steady pressure along your eye sockets under your eyes and to the outer corners of your eyes to your temples.
4. Massage your temples and behind your ears moving down along the jaw area and under the chin and down the throat.
5. Massage your scalp as if you were shampooing, using the pads of your fingers in firm circles. Repeat several times all over your head.
6. Massage your earlobes with your thumbs and forefingers.

FINISH

Bring your hands together and rub them to warm them up. Place them over your closed eyes and let them rest there for five deep, relaxing breaths.

USING A TENNIS BALL

This massage activity uses a tennis ball to provide enough pressure to relieve tension in your muscles.

START

Mindful sitting against a wall

CUES

1. Place a tennis ball just below shoulder level against the wall. If the ball slips down, place it in a sock and hold the end of the sock.
2. Perform slow, relaxing breaths when moving the tennis ball.
3. With the tennis ball against the top to middle level of your shoulder blades, slowly move it across your back, up and down the sides of your spine and in slow circles.
4. If you discover a knot, gently lean back against the tennis ball to apply pressure to the tense area.

FINISH

Take a few moments to rest and note how you feel after this massage activity.

Note: This activity can be done lying down, but it is easier to control the pressure of the ball against a wall. Instead of moving the ball, you can place the ball anywhere on your back where there is tension and hold it in place for one to two minutes.

Physical Activity

Probably nothing is more effective at managing stress than physical activity. Physical movement acts as a natural antidote to stress by increasing circulation and metabolism and balancing endocrine hormone levels. The "feel-good" hormones serotonin, dopamine, and norepinephrine, along with beta-endorphins, are released during sustained physical activity. Acute stress is not as harmful when the glucose released is used up to fuel physical exertion. Physical activity can decrease mild to moderate symptoms of depression, improve your mood, and make you less anxious. After a stressful day, instead of reaching for an alcoholic beverage, eating a high-fat snack, or taking a nap, consider playing pickup basketball or taking a Zumba fitness dance or yoga class, all of which have been favorite physical activities to combat stress reported by students. Any type of sustained moderate- to vigorous-intensity physical activity is good as long as you do it consistently most days of the week for 30 minutes and enjoy it. Check your campus recreation department for classes and activities.

Many people who are successful at sticking to a fitness regime find that the best time to exercise is the morning. Mornings generally have fewer distractions or interruptions to sideline physical activity. Moreover, the sense of accomplishment that comes after completing your fitness goals can influence your mood for the rest of the day. The key is finding the best time for you. Keep in mind that the body is meant to move, especially after being inactive (e.g., after sleeping).

Numerous factors explain why physical activity is such an effective stress management tool. These factors seem to make people more resistant to the adverse effects of stress (Salmon, 2001). Participation in physical activity buffers stress by doing the following (Southwick, Vythilingam, & Charney, 2005):

- Releasing endorphins and serotonin, which results in a state of calm and increased alertness
- Improving sleep and overall health and energy levels
- Boosting energy, increasing confidence, and establishing an internal locus of control
- Diminishing feelings of anger or frustration through physical exertion
- Providing oxygen to the brain resulting in improved cognitive functioning
- Stretching muscles that may be cramped from sitting all day
- Providing a flow experience (loss of a sense of time and self-consciousness)
- Metabolizing the circulating cortisol, glucose, and fat released in the fight or flight response
- Increasing the discipline to meet challenges
- Increasing body heat and circulation to decrease pain and release muscle tension
- Training the body to become stronger to meet the demands of stress (i.e., a stronger heart and more efficient cardiovascular system)
- Improving the function of many organs affected by the stress response and helping them to return to allostasis more efficiently
- Providing a time-out—a way to get away that is stress relieving such as being outdoors, being social, or listening to music

@ WEB LINKS

Physical Activity

- American College of Sports Medicine. This professional organization advocates for physical activity and reports on research on the science of physical activity and exercise. www.acsm.org
- American Council on Exercise. This nonprofit organization educates about the benefits of and motivation for lifelong physical activity. www.acefitness.org
- NO MORE EXCUSES—Connecting Connectors. This Facebook page was created by an international support group whose mission is to help people achieve better health and fitness with the mantra NO MORE EXCUSES. Sponsored by a life coach, it offers daily inspirational quotes from experts and others. www.facebook.com/home.php#!/pages/NO-MORE-EXCUSES-Connecting-Connectors/79368192223?fref=ts

COMMITTING TO REGULAR PHYSICAL ACTIVITY

In this activity, take the time to fully explore your physical fitness goals and the barriers you face in meeting those goals.

START

Mindful sitting with journal

CUES

1. Reflect on the benefits of physical activity for you personally.
2. Brainstorm the barriers you face to committing to regular physical activity.
3. Brainstorm ways to increase your physical activity within your lifestyle—things you can fit into your day such as doing errands on foot rather than by car.
4. Reflect on how enjoying physical activity contributes to stress management.

FINISH

Write an action step you are willing to commit to. Finish this sentence: *I will* _____.

PHYSICAL ACTIVITY LOG

In this activity you keep a physical activity log.

START

Use the physical activity log provided in the appendix.

CUES

Use the Physical Activity Log handout from the appendix to keep track of your activities for a week.

1. In the log rate how hard you worked out (intensity) and how much you enjoyed the activity.
2. Think about the support you had to complete the activity (e.g., a workout partner).
3. Consider any barriers to completing the activity (e.g., it was raining and you could not do the full 30 minutes you planned).

Physical Activity Log

Date	Physical activity (What did you do?)	Intensity level: mild (0-4); moderate (5-7); high (8-10)	Length (minutes)	Enjoyment level (0 = none; 10 = a lot)	Support	Barriers

From N. Tummers, 2013, *Stress Management: A Wellness Approach* (Champaign, IL: Human Kinetics).

The Physical Activity Log can be found in the appendix.

FINISH

At the end of a typical week (try not to use the week of exams or during holidays), set a goal to increase your physical activity the following week by increasing the frequency, increasing the intensity, spending more time, or doing a different type of physical activity. Reflect on how you feel as you make physical activity part of your lifestyle. Can you be active most days of the week?

Relaxation

The benefits of consciously taking the time to practice relaxation are numerous. This is different from kicking back in front of the TV. The relaxation response is an actual technique practiced under specific conditions (Benson, 2000). According to Benson, who studied the relaxation response with thousands of patients, the following conditions help to elicit the relaxation response: a quiet environment, a comfortable position, a place to focus your awareness and attention such as your breath, and passive concentration. Passive concentration means not forcing or expecting an outcome but just allowing the process of relaxation to happen. When we elicit the relaxation response, the following happens:

- We are in parasympathetic nervous system drive, which facilitates renewal and healing.
- Our minds can more easily switch from a racing, worried state to using the whole brain. This can result in tapping into better ideas, information, and solutions—what many call "ah-ha" moments.
- We have an internal locus of control.

Progressive muscle relaxation (PMR) involves feeling the sensation of contracting the muscles in a muscle group and then fully relaxing them. Many students who are athletes, teaching physical education, or studying kinesiology find this method useful because it is a purely physical practice; paying attention to contraction and relaxation is all it is!

In PMR each contraction is held for no more than 5 seconds, but the relaxation phase after each contraction needs to be a full 30 seconds. Do yourself a favor and don't rush. Another important tip is to keep a passive attitude by not forcing yourself or striving to fully relax; instead, slowly and gently coax your muscles to loosen their grip.

This PMR method was developed by Edmond Jacobsen (1978), who noticed that patients recovering in hospital beds were often bracing themselves, or holding tension in their muscles. He believed that healing cannot happen in a contracted, tense body. He also believed that the mind could not relax if the body wasn't relaxed. When muscles are tensed, blood flow to the area is decreased and waste products such as carbon dioxide and lactic acid build up causing more tension and pain.

Some of us find it hard to relax. We may believe that relaxing means losing control, which causes anxiety. Some of us have difficulty relaxing because we have become addicted to the hormones released during stressful situations—epinephrine and norepinephrine. The release of these hormones is known as an adrenaline rush, during which the body and mind become sharp and powerful. We may become entrenched in and addicted to being hyped up and "on" 24/7, which can make relaxing seem impossible.

Give yourself permission to relax. It's important for reducing your stress level and for keeping your body and mind working properly.

When doing the following relaxation activities, give yourself full permission to adapt the cues. For example, you may choose not to close your eyes, or to wait until you are home to do the exercises.

RELAXATION POSE

There is a best way to practice relaxation—using the *relaxation pose*.

START

Lie down face up on a firm surface such as a carpeted area or using a mat on the floor. Loosen any tight clothing and remove shoes, watches, or glasses.

CUES

1. Stretch your legs out with the feet about 2 feet (60 cm) apart.
2. Bring the arms alongside the body with the hands about 4 to 6 inches (10-15 cm) away with the palms facing up.
3. Let the head be in neutral position (not turned to the side).
4. Take a few moments to let the body relax into the floor.

FINISH

Reflect on how it feels to practice relaxation pose. Is there any part of your body that needs extra attention in order to relax? Remember to take time to allow as much relaxation and stillness in the body as possible.

BODY SCAN

In this activity, the attention is focused slowly and sequentially throughout the body. You will be scanning for sensations and in some cases noting a lack of sensation in certain body areas.

START

Mindful sitting or relaxation pose

CUES

1. Congratulate yourself on taking an active role in improving your health. Set an intention to stay awake and alert during this activity.
2. Let go of critical thoughts. There is no right way to feel; give yourself permission to just be present from moment to moment.
3. Begin diaphragmatic breathing paying close attention to your breath.
4. Start scanning your body. Imagine shining a flashlight beam at the top of your head, your scalp, and then your face. Notice any areas of comfort (relaxation, warmth, softness, ease). Scan this area slowly and notice any areas of discomfort (aches, tiredness, tension, stiffness).
5. Allow the muscles that show or sometimes hide emotions and feelings to release tension; let go of the mask you may be wearing. Notice sensations without judging; just notice them. Notice how your head area feels. There is nothing you need to feel; just pay attention and notice. Let your breath be slow, easy, and smooth.
6. Continue to bring your breath to your head area. Let the area soften and relax.
7. Continue down to other areas of your body: neck and shoulders; chest and heart space; pelvis, lower abdominals, and lower back; arms and hands; legs and feet.
8. Imagine a hole in the top of your head like a whale's spout. Breathe in from the top of your head and exhale out your feet. Now try to breathe in through your feet and exhale through your head. Try this breathing pattern several more times.

SHORTENED VARIATION

As you become more aware of where you hold tension in your body, you can do a shortened version of this activity. Pay attention to the part of your body that you habitually tense up and let it come into relaxation. Practicing a body scan several times a day is a big step toward noticing tension and bringing relaxation and comfort to those areas.

FINISH

Feel your body whole and complete, not sectioned off or fragmented. Continue to enjoy the feelings of relaxation and comfort throughout your body.

PROGRESSIVE MUSCLE RELAXATION

This activity brings awareness to muscle tension through the contraction of muscle areas followed by relaxation.

START

You can do this activity in mindful sitting, but it is recommended to learn the technique first while lying down.

CUES

1. Close your eyes and remember to engage in relaxed breathing throughout this activity, even while tensing your muscles.

2. Take a few letting-go breaths, in which your exhalation is a little longer and slower than your inhalation.

3. Find your relaxing, natural breath, the breathing rhythm that makes you feel relaxed and comfortable. Take as long as necessary to find this rhythm.

4. Imagine that with each inhalation you are bringing fresh, energized oxygen to every cell of your body.

5. Imagine that with each exhalation you are letting go of any tension, sluggishness, or discomfort.

6. Bring your focus to your arms and hands.

   a. Without tensing any other part of your body, tighten both biceps by making two fists and hold them while lifting your forearms about 2 inches (5 cm) and flexing at your elbows. Use 100 percent effort and hold for a count of 5.

   b. Now completely relax your arms and release your clenched fists. Take a deep, relaxing breath, and as you exhale, permit both arms and hands to become even more relaxed. Continue to completely relax for 25 more seconds.

   c. Repeat this exercise, but this time hold the tension at about 50 percent effort for a count of 5. Again, release fully and relax for about 30 seconds.

   d. Bring your focus back to both arms and tense them at about a 5 percent effort and hold for a count of 5.

   e. Fully relax both arms and hands, and pay attention to what this relaxation feels like for 25 seconds.

7. Take a few deep, relaxing breaths.

8. Bring your focus to your legs and feet.

   a. Without tensing any other parts of your body, point the toes of both feet hard and contract the quadriceps muscles (fronts of thighs). Make this tension a 100 percent effort and hold it for a count of 5.

   b. Allow your legs and feet to completely relax; gently shake them out and become as still as possible. Remain still and relaxed for 25 seconds.

   c. Repeat this exercise, but this time hold the tension at about 50 percent effort for a count of 5. Again, release fully and relax for about 30 seconds.

   d. Bring your focus back to both legs and feet; tense them at about a 5 percent level of effort for a count of 5.

   e. Fully relax both legs and feet noting what this relaxation feels like for 25 seconds.

9. Take a few deep, relaxing breaths.

10. Bring your focus to your abdominal area.

   a. Without tensing other parts of your body, contract the muscles of your abdominal area with a 100 percent effort by bringing your belly button to your spine. Hold the tension for a count of 5. Take a deep, relaxing breath, and as you exhale, allow your whole trunk area, both the front and back of your body, to completely soften and relax. Continue to completely relax for 25 more seconds.

    b. Now hold the tension at 50 percent effort for a count of 5. Completely let go of this tension and relax for 30 seconds.

    c. Bring only a 5 percent effort of contraction to your abdominal area. Hold it for a count of 5.

    d. Fully relax your abdomen for a full 30 seconds.

11. Take a few deep, relaxing breaths.

12. We will now focus on the shoulder and neck area.

    a. Without tensing any other parts of your body, shrug your shoulders as high as possible toward your ears and hold that tension at a 100 percent effort for a count of 5.

    b. With your next exhale, let your shoulders drop completely and gently shake them from side to side. Feel the sensation of complete relaxation in your shoulders and neck for a full 30 seconds.

    c. Now contract (shrug) at 50 percent effort and hold that contraction for a count of 5. Take a deep inhale and with the exhale allow your shoulders to drop and relax. Roll them front and back a few times and allow them to become still and soft for 30 seconds.

    d. Contract now at 5 percent effort and hold for a count of 5.

    e. Take a deep breath in and let it slowly out as you relax your shoulder and neck area completely. Take this time to pay attention to the sensations of relaxation in your entire body

13. Make a sincere effort to relax, soften, and become still and quiet as you enjoy the relaxation you've created in your body and mind. Know that your whole being is becoming stronger and more resilient. Notice how it feels to just allow for relaxation however it shows up in your body today. Allow yourself to feel more comfortable and still with your whole body finding relaxation in its own way without struggling or forcing. Simply extend an invitation of relaxation.

VARIATION

This same sequence can be extended to the face, chest, and back. PMR can take a considerable amount of time. Eventually you will be able to abbreviate the cues and home in on areas that are tense.

FINISH

Continue to breathe slowly and relax as you gently stretch your arms and legs. Bring your attention back to the room you are in, and set an intention to stay calm and relaxed as you go about your next activity.

SYMBOL OF RELAXATION

In this activity you use a personal visualization symbol—a bird soaring, a sunset, or a cup of hot chocolate.

START

Relaxation pose or mindful sitting

CUES

1. Take three deep, relaxing breaths and set an intention to come into full relaxation for the next few minutes.

2. Invite your eyes to close, or keep a soft focus in front of you. Bring to mind a visual picture representing relaxation to you. Feel free to change it, but keep the intention on relaxation.

3. As you continue to picture your symbol in your mind's eye, enjoy the feeling of relaxation flowing throughout your mind and body.

FINISH

Take a moment to reflect on using images to help you relax. What was the most relaxing image for you? Take three more relaxing breaths and enjoy the feeling of relaxation before bringing your attention back to the room you are in and the rest of your day. Remember that, with practice, images can become powerful tools to help you come into a state of relaxation.

Sleep

The term *sleep hygiene* may sound weird, but *hygiene* refers to any consistent practices you do to be healthy. Sleep is the ultimate stress management tool. According to the National Sleep Foundation (2011), we sleep to build and repair cells after all the wear and tear we experience each day. This needs to happen daily, which is why sleeping in on the weekends after days of insufficient sleep is not as healthy as having regular, consistent sleep patterns. Sleep not only helps the body repair itself, but also helps the brain assimilate all the new information we have taken in. If the body is stressed or does not get enough restful, deep sleep (or both), the brain is not able to make new brain cells or neurons. The brain's ability to make new brain cells is called *neuroplasticity* (Amen, 2008).

Many students complain that they do not get enough sleep. This results in accidents, hospitalizations, depression, decreased immune function, hormone fluctuations, decreased metabolism, impaired memory and cognitive functioning, and just being cranky (National Sleep Foundation, 2011).

According to a survey conducted by the National Sleep Foundation (2011), 67 percent of 19- to 29-year-olds brought their cell phones into their bedrooms and used them during the time they would normally have uninterrupted sleep time. Forty-two percent of the people in this same age group were likely to text during the hour before going to sleep and subsequently did not get restful sleep, resulting in feeling sleepy the next day or driving in a drowsy state. Thirty-eight percent were awakened during their sleep by their phone's ringer. Respondents also reported less restful sleep following using laptops or computers in their bedrooms to watch videos or surf the net before going to sleep.

Be aware of your sleep and energy cycles. The typical diurnal cycle (i.e., a 24-hour period) is to be most awake during late morning and mid-evening, and least awake during the early morning and at mid-afternoon. One way to stay awake and engaged during the lowest point in the cycle is to do some physical activity.

Here are some tips for helping you get a good night's sleep:

*   Schedule physical activity to finish four hours before sleep time.
*   Minimize stimulating activities right before bed (arguments, video games, violent movies, texting).
*   Avoid taking naps.

- Use tools suggested throughout this textbook such as mindful breathing, relaxation, guided imagination, and thought stopping.

- Design a sleep ritual (as a kid you may have had one that was comforting).

- Don't get into bed until you are sleepy.

- Maintain a regular sleep schedule. Avoid "catching up" on weekends. Use an alarm both to wake you up and to remind you that it's time to go to sleep.

- Put worries and your to-do list out of sight. Take time to write down your worries and then make a sincere effort to let them go.

- Avoid the trap of using alcohol to help you to sleep and caffeine to wake you up. Both can severely interfere with restful sleep.

- Use sound or music to relax. Sound machines and quiet fans can block out environmental noise.

- Take a warm shower or bath before bed, and keep your feet warm.

- Keep your bedroom cool and dark.

- Use affirmation statements such as *I am calm and relaxed.*

- Use your bed for sleeping, not as an eating area or a study space.

- Expose yourself to natural light during the day.

- Drink warm milk or soy milk with honey and vanilla before sleep to increase serotonin.

- Turn off electronics including your TV, computer, and cell phone.

SLEEP LOG

This activity involves maintaining a sleep log for one week.

START

Fill out the log provided in the appendix.

CUES

Try to be as specific as possible in your sleep log. Note any variables that might influence the quality and amount of your sleep including deadlines for classes and using relaxation methods before falling asleep.

FINISH

After one week, reflect on the amount and quality of your sleep. Consider setting a goal to change one thing about your sleep habits, such as turning off your cell phone when you go to bed.

The Sleep Log can be found in the appendix.

Qigong and Tai Chi

Qigong (pronounced "chee gung") is an ancient system of stress management that balances physical and mental energy. The benefits of qigong include strengthening and healing the body and mind, balancing emotions, and increasing energy. Qigong is just one of the many movement forms practiced extensively throughout Asia and is gaining popularity in the West. Qigong and tai chi (another movement form) are grounded in the concept that illness and disease result when chi, or energy, becomes blocked, choked, or stagnant. When the body is tense as a result of stress, breath and movement can permit the flow of positive energy and dissipate negative energy and tension. The qigong activity involves focused breathing, visualization, and a strong posture with specific body movements.

⊙ FOCUS on Research

Qigong and Tai Chi

Roger Jahnke, from the Institute of Integral Qigong and Tai Chi (Santa Barbara, California), teamed with researchers from Arizona State University and the University of North Carolina to review 66 randomized controlled research studies of tai chi and qigong involving 6,410 participants (Jahnke et al., 2010). They discovered that both tai chi and qigong improved bone health, cardiopulmonary fitness, balance, quality of life, and self-efficacy.

DIAMOND BREATH

This activity uses movement to help you connect to and lengthen your inhale and exhale.

START

Standing with your arms at your sides

CUES

1. As you inhale, slowly move both your arms out to the sides and in front to meet at eye level. Bring your thumbs and index fingers together to form a diamond shape.

2. Focusing on the diamond, slowly exhale as you gently bend your knees a few inches (or centimeters), and slowly drop the diamond to your belly button.

3. Stop and take a deep inhale and exhale here.

4. On your next inhale, slowly straighten your knees and move the diamond back to eye level and give it your full attention. Repeat 10 more times focusing on slow movement and the breath while maintaining your focus on the diamond's slow movement.

FINISH

Stand with your arms at your sides. Check in on how you are feeling and the flow of energy in your body.

PLAYING WITH ENERGY

This activity allows for the playful sensing and moving of energy.

START

Stand tall with your feet wider than your hips and your knees slightly bent. Engage your core muscles and notice how much more stable and strong your stance is.

CUES

1. Take a few deep, relaxing breaths. Throughout this activity, you will use relaxed breathing.

2. Close your eyes and take a body scan. Tune in to your body and notice where you might be feeling any discomfort, pain, or stress. Continue to take deep, relaxing breaths.

3. Bring both hands together, one on top of the other, to rest at your lower belly. Feel your breath moving against your hands for six full, deep diaphragmatic breaths. Inhale through your nose and exhale silently through slightly pursed lips.

4. Keeping your eyes closed, imagine that you are now holding a small round ball (about the size of a softball) in front of the center of your body (just above your belly button and about 8 in., or 20 cm, away). Notice the shape and color of this ball. Notice how your hands move with your breath.

5. Now with each breath, allow the ball to gradually become bigger as if you were making a huge snowball. Notice the connection of your breath to the ball. Slowly allow the ball to take on a bigger shape; what do you notice about the shape and color now? Remember to stand tall and keep your shoulders relaxed. Make sure your breath is connected to making the ball bigger and more colorful.

6. Pull the ball into your center and again bring one hand to rest on top of the other on your belly. Feel your hands move with your breath. Take five more deep belly breaths. Notice how you feel right now. What do you notice? What is the energy like in your body?

@ WEB LINKS

Sleep

- National Heart Lung and Blood Institute. This U.S. government agency provides health information for the public including information on sleep disorders. www.nhlbi.nih.gov/health/index.htm
- National Sleep Foundation. This website offers all you can ever want to know about the effects of sleep and sleep deprivation on health including improving-your-brain games. www.sleepfoundation.org

Tai Chi

- Beginner tai chi video. www.youtube.com/watch?v=P5hvODK2zW4
- Gaiam. This company is an excellent source of tai chi, yoga, and other physical activity DVDs as well as other products for health and wellness. www.gaiam.com/text/home/about-gaiam.htm

7. Release your hands to the sides of your body. Slowly allow your chin to drop into your chest, lengthening your cervical spine. On the inhale, imagine that you are pulling your breath up from the center of your body, up your spine and into your heart space, and continue to pull your breath up into your head. As you breathe out, direct your exhale back toward the center of your body. Continue to pull the in-breath up your spine into your head and the out-breath back down into your core for five more breath cycles.

8. Come back to regular, relaxed breathing and slowly lift your head and stand up tall. Slowly open your eyes.

9. Taking deep breaths, gently tap (with your fingers or cupped palms) your chest, then your scalp, and then around your eyes.

10. Tap from your shoulder down along the top of the arm to your fingers with the palm of the opposite hand, and then tap back up your shoulder and around the side of your neck.

11. Repeat this three more times and then switch sides.

12. With fists or open, cupped hands, gently tap your kidney area, your hips, and down your legs to your feet. Do this four times.

13. Tap your head and then "sweep it off" as if sweeping off bad energy.

14. Tap your chest and sweep off negative energy. Then go through your arms and lower body, tapping and sweeping.

FINISH

Return to standing with your hands one on top of the other over your lower belly. Notice any changes in your body, any shift in energy or sensations.

Yoga

Yoga, another ancient system of stress management, includes the following:

- Pranayama (breath activities)
- Energizing yoga asanas or poses
- Restorative yoga asanas or poses
- Relaxation activities: body scan technique, relaxation pose

Yoga helps us manage stress by allowing for the yoking, or merging, of the spirit, mind, and body. Yoga is not merely exercise but a practice focused on becoming stronger, strengthening the breath, releasing tension, building awareness and mindfulness, encouraging positive imagery and thinking, and committing to self-

@ WEB LINKS

Yoga

- American Yoga Association. This organization offers resources for yoga instruction and information. www.americanyogaassociation.org/contents.html
- *Yoga Journal.* This print and online resource publishes articles on yoga poses, the benefits of yoga, and places to practice yoga. www.yogajournal.com

care. The bridge that brings about this yoking is the breath. Yoga is practiced with a dedication to being in a state of relaxed breathing.

Here are some tips to keep in mind while practicing yoga.

- Take your time to set up and "grow" each asana or pose. Yoga is the one place in which you do not need to be in a hurry.

- Always work from a strong foundation; this includes alignment and awareness of breathing while standing, seated, twisted, and lying down.

- Maintain a moment-to-moment awareness without striving or judging. Give yourself permission to be just the way you are.

- Keep exploring what is called in yoga "the edge," or middle path. Practice the poses with enough effort to allow for growth but without pushing or harming. Keep asking these questions: Is the sensation I am feeling good for me? Am I encouraging growth, or is this feeling a signal to modify or come out of the pose? Is my breath with me in the pose? Am I practicing from a place of deep consideration for my body?

- Commit to an attitude of *ahimsa*, a Sanskrit word meaning "nonharming." If we take it one step further in terms of our mindfulness practice, it means paying attention, listening, honoring, and taking care of our bodies, hearts, and minds as a whole, and seeking health and healing.

- Allow your breath and body to provide feedback. Take the time to listen and stay awhile in the pose. Allow for emotions and thoughts to bubble to the surface, but choose to stay grounded and centered in your yoga practice right now and not to react.

COBRA POSE

The cobra pose is a core strengthener. In cobra, the hands are not doing the work; they are more for balance. (See figure 2.3.)

START

Prone (lying flat on the floor on your belly)

CUES

1. Bring your legs together like the tail of a snake. Keep your lower body strong and grounded into the floor.

2. Place your hands at your chest line under your shoulders, fingers pointed forward with elbows bent and close to the sides of your ribs.

FIGURE 2.3 Cobra pose.

3. Press your hands into the floor and gently lift your chest keeping your head in line with your spine (do not extend your back). Feel the stretch in your back while looking straight ahead.

4. Keeping your lower body strong and grounded into the floor and your back fluid, open up the front of your body.

5. Hold cobra pose for five breaths.

FINISH

Gently come out of cobra and continue to lie prone for a few relaxing breaths.

WARRIOR I POSE

Warrior I is a total body strengthening exercise: the legs hold the pose, the arms reach overhead, and the core is engaged to keep the pose steady and the spine strong. (See figure 2.4.)

START

Standing with feet hip-width apart

CUES

1. Take a big step back with your left foot about 3 feet (1 m) into a lunge. Your right foot should be straight ahead with the knee bent. Your left foot should be turned out to the side slightly (the right foot points at 12 o'clock and the left foot points at 9 or 10 o'clock).

2. Square your shoulders and hips to the front.

3. Reach overhead with strong arms, and keep your back leg as straight and strong as possible.

4. Hold this pose for five breaths.

5. Step back to standing and repeat on the opposite leg.

FINISH

Rest quietly while standing.

FIGURE 2.4 Warrior I pose.

TREE POSE

The tree pose is a quintessential balancing pose in yoga that looks easy but can be a challenge! (See figure 2.5.)

START

Standing with feet together

CUES

1. Stand tall and strong and place your weight on one leg. Pretend that your standing foot has grown roots into the earth below and the top of your head is reaching to the sun. Now bring the sole of the other foot to rest on the inner calf muscle, inner thigh, or on the top of the supporting foot.

2. Bring your hands to your heart space and slowly grow the branches of the tree (reaching your arms up to the sky or out to the sides). Make sure to breathe and keep your eyes trained on a spot in front of you.

3. Hold tree pose for five breaths or more.

4. Switch feet. You can use a chair or the wall for help balancing.

FINISH

Stand with your feet together. Take a moment to check in with how you feel after practicing tree pose. Was there a difference between sides? Our trees tend to be stronger on our dominant leg. It is important to practice and strengthen both sides.

FIGURE 2.5   Tree pose.

DOWNWARD FACING DOG POSE

This pose allows for inversion—that is, the heart is higher than the head, which can promote relaxation. (See figure 2.6.)

START

On the floor on your hands and knees in table top pose

FIGURE 2.6   Downward facing dog pose.

CUES

1. Place your hands shoulder-width apart and flat on the floor straight ahead with your fingers spread wide and strong.

2. Curl your toes under and balance on the balls of your feet while keeping your feet hip-width apart.

3. Straighten your legs and lift your hips up into an inverted-V shape. Lift your buttock muscles and tailbone high and back. Your heels do not need to touch the ground, but try to let them sink deeply toward the floor.

4. Hold downward dog for five breaths.

5. Relax your head and look toward your knees; press your chest back toward strong legs.

FINISH

Gently release both legs, coming back into table top pose.

SEATED TWIST POSE

This pose allows for the core to be gently twisted, releasing tension. (See figure 2.7.)

START

Seated on the floor with legs straight out in front

CUES

1. Keeping one leg glued to the floor and sitting tall, bend your other knee to place your foot flat on the floor.

2. Twist by turning your belly button toward your bent knee. Bring your opposite elbow across your body and hook it on the outside of your knee, or turn and hug the outside of your knee. Hold this for five deep, relaxing breaths.

3. Come back to center. Switch legs.

FINISH

Gently bring both legs together in front and shake them out.

FIGURE 2.7   Seated twist pose.

CHILD POSE

Use this pose to come into a relaxing time-out.

START
Sitting on the floor on your knees

CUES
1. Bring your buttocks to rest on your heels.
2. Rest your forehead on the floor in front, or make a platform with one fist on top of the other and rest your forehead on your stacked fists.
3. Put your arms out in front, or place them alongside your body.

FINISH
Notice how relaxing in child pose helps you to become calm. (See figure 2.8.)

FIGURE 2.8   Child pose.

Summary

This chapter focused on physical wellness and stress management activities with a physical approach. The physical dimension of wellness addresses many areas from nutrition to breathing to physical fitness and sleep, as well as ways to reduce the risk of physical harm such as alcohol poisoning. Try the activities described here and see how they fit into your lifestyle—that is, the things you do consistently either every day or most days of the week.

Many students make the mistake of trying to do too much at one time. Small changes can make a world of difference. What is important is making a commitment for consistency. Consider practicing one physical stress management activity for a week. For example, purchase a pedometer that measures how many you steps you take and try to increase your step count each week. This small step (bad pun) can make a big impact by helping you to have more restful sleep and to feel more alert. This, in turn, might motivate you to take another small step toward health and happiness such as quitting smoking. Chapter 3 focuses on emotional stress and stress management activities that address it.

stress

chapter 3

Emotional Wellness

This being human is a guest house.
Every morning a new arrival.
A joy, a depression, a meanness,
some momentary awareness comes
as an unexpected visitor.
Welcome and entertain them all!
Even if they are a crowd of sorrows,
who violently sweep your house
empty of its furniture,
still, treat each guest honorably.
He may be clearing you out
for some new delight.
The dark thought, the shame, the malice,
meet them at the door laughing and invite them in.
Be grateful for whatever comes,
because each has been sent
as a guide from beyond.

Jelaluddin Rumi, translation by Coleman Barks

What is emotional wellness? People who are emotionally well are aware of and act proactively and in health-enhancing ways to all emotions. An emotionally well person also is able to recognize and empathize with the emotions of others. They generally exhibit the health-enhancing qualities of optimism, self-regulation (not flipping out or being nasty toward others when emotionally upset), self-worth and confidence, empathy, and compassion. They solve problems, form positive relationships, and persevere through difficulty (Seligman, 2011).

According to Howard Gardner (1983), all of us exhibit strengths in at least one kind of intelligence. We often think of intelligence as being smart in academics, but emotional intelligence is a form of intelligence that enables people to recognize emotions and act in positive ways as well as empathize with or understand the emotions others are feeling. Gardner believes that emotions give meaning and purpose to life. They are messengers, and what we choose to do with these messages is critical. When we have an internal locus of control, we are not controlled by the past (guilt) or by the future (worry and fear); we understand, rather, that the only thing within our control is the ability to be present. Being aware of and experiencing our feelings enables us to manage how we will respond. We can pay attention to our emotions as motivation for positive actions and focus on using our strengths when we feel challenged and vulnerable (O'Connor, 2005).

By practicing staying in the present moment and being mindful of our emotions (mindfulness is discussed in more detail in chapter 4), we can avoid focusing on outcomes (worry about the future) or how we messed up last time (guilt about the past). We often choose these familiar habits rather than take the time and effort to become aware of the way emotions stress us, and to use stress management tools. The following list presents some thoughts on enhancing emotional wellness.

- The groundwork of improving emotional intelligence is awareness. This means monitoring yourself when you become distracted. As the poem by Rumi that starts this chapter indicates, we need to embrace all emotions and practice emotional regulation (Goleman, 2011).

- When we are relaxed and centered, we are better able to manage our emotions. When we can breathe and be mindful, we shift to gamma wave connections in the right hemisphere of the brain and are able to tap into more insight and better actions (Goleman, 2011).

- From a place of awareness, we can look to the message of our emotional reaction to understand what is causing it. For example: *My [emotional reaction] is a reminder of what I need to do.*

- Once we understand the message of the emotion, we can choose a response—how or whether to act. Emotions and behaviors are two separate things.

- Moods are enduring emotional states. Sometimes it is hard to pinpoint what triggers our moods. They can be affected by our state of health, the friends we are with, and even the weather. When you find yourself in a funk, can you wait on making decisions on important issues until you are in a better place?

- Emotional wellness, or emotional intelligence, is not only about an awareness of and ability to manage our own emotions. It also involves being aware of and empathizing with the emotions of others. We address emotions within our relationships by using the skills of listening, cooperating, and resolving conflict (Goleman, 2000, 2011).

@ WEB LINKS

Emotional Wellness

- Six Seconds: Emotional intelligence for Positive Change. This organization offers information on training in emotional intelligence including research on children and adults. www.6seconds.org

- Edutopia. This organization, founded by George Lucas, has outstanding videos educating about an important component of education: social and emotional learning. www.edutopia.org/video

- Multiple Intelligences for Adult Literacy and Education. On this site you can find out your strengths in terms of Gardner's' multiple intelligences. The site provides ideas and resources for improving each area of intelligence. www.literacyworks.org/mi/intro/index.html

- Jed Foundation. This is the leading organization in the United States promoting emotional intelligence and preventing suicide on college campuses. www.jedfoundation.org

EMOTIONAL STRENGTHS OF A ROLE MODEL

In this activity you reflect on a person you believe to be emotionally healthy and consider some of their behaviors that you might want to practice.

START

Mindful sitting with journal

CUES

1. Reflect on someone you know who you believe is emotionally healthy.
2. Write down the personal characteristics of this person that convey emotional health.
3. Compare these characteristics to those discussed in the strengths-based approach section in chapter 1.
4. Reflect on ways you might adopt one or more of these characteristics.

FINISH

Notice how you feel when thinking about this person and how he or she has inspired you to be more emotionally healthy.

Feel it, identify it, accept and understand it, be authentic to yourself, and use a stress management tool.

Goleman, 2000

TAKING IT TO HEART

This activity invites you to sit with difficult emotions in a heart-centered space and be less critical and judgmental.

START

Mindful sitting

CUES

1. Take a moment to settle into a comfortable posture that allows for you to feel centered and grounded. Take as many deep and restful breaths as you need to feel relaxed and calm.
2. Notice any emotions that you may be experiencing at this time. Notice in particular any dark, gloomy, or troubling emotions.
3. Can you bring an intention of awareness, light, and caring to these dark areas? Shine this light on any distressing feeling you are trying to avoid or stuff away.
4. Be aware of and curious about how your body responds to this situation.
5. Bring your awareness to the area around your heart. Notice this area with kindness and compassion. Imagine that you are breathing in and out of your heart space.

6. For just a while, in your heart space, permit yourself to consider how it might feel to be less critical and judgmental of this situation. Can you acknowledge how it feels to concede to just a little letting go?

FINISH

Reflect on how shifting your attitude toward and taking to heart this situation felt even for just a few breaths. Did something surface that was meaningful to you?

HITTING THE PAUSE BUTTON

This heart-based stress management activity is adapted from Dr. Childre's book *The HeartMath Solution* (Childre, Martin, & Beech, 2000). The Institute of HeartMath, founded by Dr. Childre, is a nonprofit organization promoting heart-based research, which includes the principle of entrainment. Entrainment involves shifting from a stressful perception and aligning the distressed brain-wave rhythms with the calming, centered, and more emotionally intelligent rhythms of the heart. In this way, the body and mind can work more efficiently with decreased stress and anxiety. (See the Web Links: Heart Math sidebar and visit the website for more information about the Institute of HeartMath.)

START

Mindful sitting

CUES

1. Think about a personal problem you are having. Notice your physical and emotional perceptions when considering this situation. Imagine you are viewing this problem as an image on a high-definition screen in your mind's eye. Take a few more moments to focus on this scene. Now imagine you are hitting a pause button and putting this image aside for a moment.

2. Focus on relaxed, natural breathing as you shift your awareness to the area around your heart. Imagine you are breathing in and out of your heart for five relaxed and comfortable breaths; imagine your heart area getting more spacious with each breath. Connect with the heart as you slow your heart rate. Feel your body relax as you breathe in and out of your heart space.

3. Recall a positive experience in which you had a strong, positive emotion such as gratitude, joy, happiness, or love. What was it like to experience this positive emotion? Take five relaxing and comfortable breaths as you recall and enjoy this positive experience.

4. Ask your heart what might be a more positive and effective way to deal with the problem you paused. Try to view this problem through the intention of an open heart.

5. Listen to your heart and determine an action step you can take to respond to this problem.

FINISH

Take some time now to reflect on this exercise. You can draw, write, or talk with someone you trust about the problem and possible action steps, including not doing anything.

Based on Childre and Martin 1999.

Happiness

Happiness can be a difficult concept to define. It is a universal desire, but what causes happiness varies among cultures. According to Martin Seligman, who has studied happiness extensively, a better term for happiness is *well-being*. The term *well-being* includes the following elements (Seligman, 2011, p. 16):

- Positive emotion
- Engagement
- Positive relationships
- A sense of meaning (i.e., belonging to and serving something)
- Feelings of accomplishment

The "pursuit of happiness" may sound like a shopping trip—looking outside ourselves to find something to make us happy (e.g., the newest iPhone, Nike shoes). Increasing or cultivating happiness requires that we discover what makes us happy within. *Cultivating* means not only planting the seeds of happiness, but also nurturing them.

According to researchers, we have a happiness set point that we fall back to, but this can be increased. Sonja Lyubomirksy, at the University of California at Riverside, is a researcher, professor, and author of *The How of Happiness* (2007). She believes that 40 percent of our capacity for happiness can be developed. Even though life situations have very little to do with being happy, we direct a lot of our energy, time, and money into these things, Lyubomirsky asserts. Despite what we think, winning the lottery may make a person happy for a while, but after a certain point, that person resets back to his or her normal level, or set point, of happiness.

Lyubomirsky, King, and Diener (2005) conducted an intensive meta-analysis of research of happiness, or positive affect. They reviewed 293 study groups with over

@ WEB LINKS

Heart Math

Institute of HeartMath. This nonprofit research and education organization investigates the relationships among stress reduction, self-regulation of emotions, and resilience. www.heartmath.org

Happiness

- Authentic Happiness. Martin Seligman's website is a great resource for self-reported questionnaires to help people learn more about themselves and the measures of the strengths-based approach to wellness. www.authentichappiness.sas.upenn.edu/Default.aspx
- Positive Psychology Center. This research center investigates strengths-based approaches that help people to flourish. It promotes scientific research, offers training, and provides information about the field of positive psychology. www.positivepsychology.org
- Track Your Happiness. This project offers a cell phone app that tracks situations or times of happiness. It also offers suggestions for increasing happiness. www.trackyourhappiness.org

Supportive friends, classmates, and coworkers can help carry the workload, increasing the room in your life for happiness.

275,000 participants. They found that happy people were more likely than their less happy peers to have fulfilling relationships, higher incomes, success in their work, community involvement, physical health, and longevity. Their research concluded that the following can increase happiness:

- Seeking positive social support and activities
- Being generous with one's time, energy, and enthusiasm, to oneself and others, including volunteering
- Having a positive perception of self and others: practicing unconditional love and loving-kindness
- Seeking contentment and peace
- Solving problems and being creative
- Being likeable and cooperative (playing nice with others!)
- Practicing positive coping and healthy behaviors
- Practicing being mindful and appreciating being present with others
- Toning down criticisms of self and others

MY HAPPINESS PROJECT

Sonja Lyubomirsky (2007) and Gretchen Rubin, the author of *The Happiness Project* (2009), have outlined a weekly or monthly practice to increase happiness in your life.

START

The following is a list of activities to try for a week (or other specific amount of time) (Lyubomirsky, 2007):

- Be grateful.
- Be positive.
- Seek out social connections.
- Commit to a goal—pursue a passion.
- Be mindful—pay attention to what you do and say.
- Be forgiving.
- Seek out flow experiences (activities in which you lose yourself and play).
- Find meaning and purpose in what you do and say.
- Do more enjoyable physical activity.
- Meditate.

Make a short list of activities for your happiness project that would be the most enjoyable, easily could be part of your lifestyle, and are of value to you.

CUES

Pick one activity that you are motivated and committed to pursuing. Find a method to keep track of your progress such as journal or a chart.

FINISH

Make sure to reflect on how your experience of happiness is changing.

Based on Lyubomirsky 2007.

PLANTING THE SEEDS OF HAPPINESS

This activity is a reminder that we are all responsible for our own happiness; no one else can make us happy, and conversely, we cannot make someone else happy.

START

Mindful sitting

CUES

1. Take a few moments to relax and breathe, imagining inhaling and exhaling from your heart center. Make a sincere effort to zero in on your well-being.
2. Reflect on experiences in your life you wish to savor, or take the time to appreciate an experience in which you were joyful or had fun. Try to describe what you were feeling during this time.
3. Sit for a few moments allowing this experience to permeate each of your cells with the feelings you felt.

FINISH

Notice how reflecting on feelings of joy, fun, and happiness color the rest of your day.

Laughter

During a period of intense stress, you might have been surprised at how humor makes its way into the picture to relieve some of the tension. A good belly laugh can be seen as an internal workout, decreasing stress hormones, improving the immune system, oxygenizing the blood, and making the diaphragm and abdominal

Laughter Yoga

Laughter Yoga International is a foundation dedicated to combining unconditional laughter with yoga breathing. It can feel a little strange at first to stand with others in a circle and just laugh for no reason. However, the body doesn't know whether the laughter is genuine or fake; it just reaps the benefits. Eventually, the laughter becomes infectious, much like yawning, and you can't help yourself! There are laughter clubs all over the world—social groups that get together to just laugh, and memberships and meetings are always free! http://laughteryoga.org

muscles work. Using humor to deal with stress is part of human nature. It can be a way to see hope in the middle of chaos, to share with others some lightness, and to release toxins and stress. Have you ever laughed until you cried?

Norman Cousins was a medical doctor frustrated with the lack of improvement in his own health. In his book *Anatomy of an Illness* (1979), he emphasized the importance of laughter and humor when he was dealing with his own recovery from heart disease. In fact, his practice of using laughter to heal himself became a case study in a major medical journal. He loved to watch the Marx Brothers, whom he considered to be geniuses of comedy in their day (1930-1950s) and are still popular today. Many hospitals now have laughter rooms and clowns in residence. Companies use humor therapy to improve employee motivation.

There are many forms of humor including black, potty, parody, and irony. It is important to emphasize that not all humor is funny. When humor makes fun of or puts down a specific group, is at the expense of someone else's feelings, is offensive, or makes us feel superior to others, it can cause distress in others or make a situation worse.

KEEPING A HUMOR PORTFOLIO

A humor portfolio is a collection of your favorite ways to laugh and keep a sense of humor during stressful circumstances. This portfolio can include jokes, videos, quotes from movies, photos, puns, or descriptions of situations. Try your hand at making your own jokes or comic materials. Set a goal to find something humorous each day and to not take things so seriously. Be open to the lighter side of life.

Art Healing

Art healing, or art therapy, which focuses on expressing emotions nonverbally, can be an incredible tool for stress management—a picture paints a thousand words. It is important to emphasize that making art in this context is not about creating a product (e.g., a work of art); rather, it is about the process itself. At first students often scoff at their ability to do art until it is pointed out all the ways they do so, by drawing doodles and other shapes, patterns, and pictures. Paying attention to these symbols can be a powerful way to understand and process stress. In art healing, we pay attention to the colors we choose as well as the symbols or icons we use often or gravitate toward. Once you have drawn something, give yourself time to interpret it. What is it saying to you? Keep in mind that there is no right way to create art; it is all good. The meaning you give to your creation is key and part of the healing process. Therefore, make sure to try out all of your ideas, avoid any competition or comparison to others' work, suspend judgment, and honor your right to not share your work with others.

In our digital age of clip art and cutting and pasting images, we may have lost the chance to create with hands-on materials! When you are making art, be sure to have a variety of color choices in as many mediums as possible (e.g., crayons, ink, colored pencils, finger paint, colored pastels, and paint). Modeling clay is also an option. Using blank newsprint is an economical way to create as much art as possible. Bring in fabric, beads, or "found" objects (from nature or found on the street) to add to the richness and texture of your work.

Following are some suggested forms of art to explore:

- Self-portrait—Who am I?
- Peaceful scenes, healing images, or dream impressions
- Mandalas (circles that include sacred and meaningful images; Cornell, 2006)
- Emotional masks (How might you hide, or mask, your true feelings or emotions?)
- Collages of your emotional states

Dealing With Difficult Emotions

In our busy world, we seldom take the time to explore our feelings; we are more inclined to hide from them, repress them, or express them in unhealthy ways. We do not accept our emotions for a variety of reasons, including not considering them important, confusing them with thoughts, or not being aware of them. Not acknowledging our feelings can cause stress and have detrimental effects on all aspects of wellness. For example, repressing a feeling of grief is stressful because the mind and body need to express this loss to heal from it.

Art can be a creative outlet for expressing your emotions.

Certain emotions such as worry, guilt, anger, and fear can make us more susceptible to the effects of stress. When these emotions become habitual responses, to the point of becoming part of our personality, our health deteriorates. Four basic personality types relate to how individuals deal with stressors (Miller, 2005). The key issue is the concept of locus of control, which was discussed in chapter 1. Locus of control refers to our attitude toward stressful situations. If we believe we have power and choices, we have an internal locus of control. If we feel hopeless, victimized, dependent, and out of control in a situation we believe is out of our hands, we have an external locus of control.

- Type A personality has the characteristics of being always in a hurry, competitive, driven, and prone to multitasking. Type A people feel empowered by an internal locus of control; they get things done. These behaviors can be sources of stress if they are not balanced with stress management practices such as relaxation and mindfulness.

- Type B personality is characterized by being relaxed, easygoing, and not easily stressed. A person with this personality type may seem to be a poster child for stress management. However, type B people have an external locus of control; they often adopt the attitude that someone other than them is going to get things done or tell them what to do. As a result, they often take no action and procrastinate. The stress may actually land more on the people who have to work with type B people than on the type B people themselves. Moreover, their work is often done at the last minute and of poor quality. It is important for those who have type B tendencies to make sure to have an action plan for important responsibilities and commit to following through on the plan.

- Type C is characterized by being nonassertive and letting others make decisions. This translates into an external locus of control associated with a sense of hopelessness and victimization. People with this personality type are vulnerable to depression. Those with type C characteristics could use the various activities in this chapter for coping with difficult emotions and doing as much as possible to foster an internal locus of control.

- Type D, or distressed personality, is characterized as chronically experiencing and suppressing negative emotions such as uncontrolled hostility and aggression. Additionally, people with this personality type have a tendency to become socially isolated (Miller, 2005). Feeling helplessness and hopelessness,

@ WEB LINKS

Mandalas

The Mandala Project. This nonprofit organization is dedicated to promoting peace through art and education. www.mandalaproject.org

Dealing With Difficult Emotions

- Queendom. This site, sponsored by the Discovery channel, provides quizzes about health-related issues including anxiety, assertiveness, and optimism. http://discoveryhealth.queendom.com

- Live Your Life Well. This nonprofit organization's webpage is sponsored by Mental Health America and offers tools to help cope with stress. www.liveyourlifewell.org

these people have an external locus of control and are vulnerable to illness including coronary artery disease. This personality type would do well to seek out friends they can confide in and practice dealing proactively with negative emotions as much as possible without reverting to anger.

PERSONALITY AND STRESS MANAGEMENT SMALL-GROUP ACTIVITY

This activity allows for students to come up with ways to deal proactively with potentially harmful personality types and suggests which stress management activities each personality type could use.

START

Students will work in small groups of three or four students per group.

CUES

1. Take a few moments to discuss the four different personality types and reflect on people in your life in whom you recognize these personality characteristics. Students do not need to disclose any names but can say "I know someone who . . ."

2. Discuss as a group how these personality types might be detrimental to health. Offer examples of what you might have experienced as a result of this personality type.

3. Discuss what stress management practices you would suggest to each of the personality types in order for them to have healthier and balanced lives.

FINISH

After the small-group activity, individuals can reflect on whether they have any of the personality type characteristics and what stress management activities they might be willing to practice to become healthier and more balanced.

Anger

"Anger is an emotion characterized by antagonism toward someone or something you feel has deliberately done you wrong" (American Psychological Association, n.d.b). Anger can be an important clue to recognizing a true violation or threat against us or another person—for example, we can become angry when our feelings are hurt. Anger can result when our needs or expectations are not met or when someone breaks one of our rules. It is important to face anger early rather than letting it fester and worsen. Anger is a temporary reaction to a specific event, whereas hostility is

@ WEB LINKS

Anger Management

- angermgmt.com. This site offers information on building better relationships. http://angermgmt.com
- American Psychological Association. Controlling Anger Before It Controls You. www.apa.org/topics/anger/control.aspx

a longer-lasting attitude motivated by hate and animosity.

Anger is caused when someone breaks a rule and provokes a reaction within you. The following are some actions you can take to change how you perceive a broken rule or unmet expectation:

- Look below the surface to what may be causing your anger.
- Be more empathetic, understanding others' behaviors and why they may not adhere to or follow the rule you feel has been broken. Reexamine the rule!
- Remove yourself from the situation so the anger doesn't escalate. Give it some space and time to pass. Count to 10. Go for a walk. Find something to occupy your attention.
- Distract yourself: exercise, listen to music, laugh.
- Steer your anger toward positive actions; be assertive.
- Look at the situation from a different perspective; get rid of unrealistic expectations.
- Let it go and forgive.

Everyone gets angry sometimes, and that's okay. How you step back, process, and then respond to that anger rather than reacting is what makes the difference.

Trying to dissipate the anger by screaming or punching a pillow actually increases the negative effects of stress reactivity, especially the release of cortisol. A better choice would be to do some physical activity.

SELF-ASSESSMENT OF AN ANGER SITUATION

This activity invites you to explore a situation that causes anger and reflect on how you might move on from this situation.

START
Mindful sitting with journal

CUES
1. Identify a situation right now that makes you angry. What were the expectations or rules someone did not meet?
2. Reflect on where anger shows up or manifests physically and emotionally.
3. Identify any other feelings that have surfaced from these unmet expectations or broken rules, such as loss or sadness.

4. Process this situation:

   a. Validate your feelings—is your reaction warranted?

   b. Explore any exaggerated feelings.

   c. Explore the reasons for these unmet expectations or broken rules.

5. Identify methods you could use to adopt an internal locus of control, such as doing a breathing exercise, reciting affirmations, setting goals, using better interpersonal communication, changing your self-talk, or using disputation (described in chapter 4). Reflect on the stress management tools you could use when confronted with this situation again.

6. See the situation from the other person's point of view. Can you be empathetic and see this person's perspective? Are you willing to consider what might have made the person break the rule or not meet your expectation in the first place? Can you own your own responsibilities for this situation?

FINISH

Reflect on your personal health and how anger affects it. What are the next steps you are willing to take to resolve this anger?

Depression

How do you know whether your sadness is normal or becoming a problem? According to the World Health Organization (WHO), "Depression is a common mental disorder, characterized by sadness, loss of interest or pleasure, feelings of guilt or low self-worth, disturbed sleep or appetite, feelings of tiredness, and poor concentration. Depression can be long-lasting or recurrent, substantially impairing an individual's ability to . . . cope with daily life. At its most severe, depression can lead to suicide. When mild, people can be treated without medicines but when depression is moderate or severe they may need medication and professional talking treatments" (WHO, 2012). It is important to note that many of the emotional wellness activities described here are used with patients in treatment for depression.

Guilt, Worry, and Anxiety

The cause of stress can often be attributed to various kinds of fear, such as the fear of rejection, the unknown, failure, loss, isolation, and loss of control. Guilt and worry are the two emotional culprits involved with almost all of our stress (Dyer, 1976).

Guilt is defined as the emotion we feel when we did not do the right thing, such as lying, breaking a promise, or intentionally hurting someone else's feelings. Guilt

@ WEB LINKS

Depression

- American Psychological Association. This site offers numerous articles on topics of mental health, including depression, stress, and stress management. www.apa.org

- American Association of Suicidology. This organization is dedicated to understanding and preventing suicide. www.suicidology.org

is focused on past behavior. A lot of stress is caused by focusing on the past, which we cannot change. However, there are things you may be able to do in the present, such as the following:

- Ask yourself: Is there something I can do to make this situation right?
- Forgive yourself and focus on what you learned from the situation.
- Stop blaming yourself.
- Decide what you can do to fix the situation, such as apologize, admit you were wrong, or make amends.

Worry is defined as being concerned about the future, especially the experience of uncertainty about what will happen. Worry causes anxiety with resulting stress reactivity and the cascade of detrimental hormones. Remember, we cannot control the future, and we often spend a lot of time and energy worrying about things we cannot control. Mark Twain once said: "I've had a lot of worries in my life, most of which never happened." Anxiety is the psychological and physiological response to overwhelming worry and fear. Here are some tips for dealing with worry and anxiety:

- Be well prepared for possible stressful situations so you don't feel powerless.
- Slow down and use your breath, relaxation, and affirmations.
- Be aware of defense mechanisms (discussed in the Common Defense Mechanisms section later in this chapter) that you might use to protect your ego or sense of self.
- Use problem solving as described in chapter 4.
- Use the skill of disputation (i.e., putting your worry to the test—also described in chapter 4).
- Stay in the present moment. Worry and fear are projections into the future and often are about things that never happen.

THE DIFFICULT EMOTIONS BIN

In this activity you physically write all your worries, feelings of guilt, and concerns on a large piece of paper, or you imagine this list in your mind's eye. This activity can be useful if your mind is racing with obligations and deadlines and you are trying to get to sleep. It can also be helpful if you tend to ruminate about issues.

START
Mindful sitting with pencil or pen, pieces of scrap paper or a journal, and a wastebasket or other large receptacle

CUES
1. Take a few deep, centering breaths.
2. Make a list of the difficult emotions that you are facing right now: any worries or guilty thoughts you have that are weighing you down (either write them down or make a mental list).
3. Now tear off each item from your list, bunch it up, and toss it into a bin—a wastebasket. With each toss, say silently to yourself, *I am letting this go.*
4. Resist the temptation to hang on to difficult emotions as you toss them into the bin; you are setting the intention right now to release them. Repeat to yourself, *Right now, I am free of difficult emotions.*

FINISH

Reflect on how it feels to let go of difficult emotions for a short period of time even if they may be important. Reflect on how letting go might be helpful so you can do proactive things such as sleeping and studying.

Fear

Fear is the emotion we feel when we are facing danger, either physical or emotional. It can be a warning of real danger such as a snarling dog about to attack, or a reaction to worry about the future. Fear is necessary for survival. We may have experienced physical fear and mobilized accordingly into fight or flight. Much of our fear, however, is not a reaction to physical threats but to threats to self-perceptions; we are afraid of being judged, abandoned, or rejected. The trouble is that our bodies react with stress reactivity whether our fear is a reaction to a real or emotional threat.

Following are some actions you can take to deal with fear:

- Admit and confront your fears.
- Call your fear something else, such as a challenge or a means to use your strengths.
- Take action.

DEALING WITH FEAR

This journal activity provides the opportunity to explore an appropriate and healthy acknowledgment of fear.

START

Mindful sitting with journal

CUES

1. Describe a situation in which you often feel fear. What can you do about this fear, and what would you like to do to move forward and come to terms with this fearful situation?
2. Is there a goal you could set to deal with this situation?
3. What action steps are you willing to take to achieve this goal right now and in the future?
4. What resources and support do you need to move forward?
5. What attitudes and other obstacles do you need to overcome to move forward?

FINISH

Take a moment to reflect on what action steps you will take to deal with this fear.

Sadness

Sadness is a feeling that comes up when we experience loss or disappointment. A healthy form of sadness is grief. An unhealthy form would be allowing the sadness to overcome your life without taking steps to resolving those feelings. This emotion is mostly associated with death, but it can arise whenever we experience loss, of a relationship, health, independence, or something we enjoy doing and can no longer do.

PROCESSING GRIEF

This journal activity provides the opportunity to explore an appropriate and healthy acknowledgment of loss, disappointment, or failure and how to move forward.

START

Mindful sitting with journal

CUES

1. Describe a loss, disappointment, or failure you have experienced.
2. Reflect on what you have learned from this experience and what you would like to do to move forward and come to terms with this situation.
3. Is there a goal you could set to deal with this situation?
4. What action steps are you willing to take to achieve this goal right now and in the future?
5. What resources and support do you need to move forward?
6. What attitudes and other obstacles do you need to overcome to move forward?

FINISH

How does it feel to take the time to process and give your grief the attention it needs as well as to move forward from it?

Defense Mechanisms

Defense mechanisms are ways we defend and protect ourselves when our sense of self is threatened or we are feeling the fight or flight response. We avoid or make excuses for our behaviors to decrease anxiety and avoid conflict. Using a defense mechanisms to divert our attention from what is bothering us can become a habit, but this can aggravate stress and block personal growth and achievement. Common defense mechanisms include:

- Denial: Denying that the situation happened
- Dependency: Relying on others to make you feel better about yourself
- Displacement: Taking negative feelings out on someone or something else
- Fantasy: Escaping into a false sense of reality
- Hopelessness: Not being optimistic or hopeful to protect against disappointment
- Intellectualization: Making excuses by overthinking and rationalizing
- Minimization: Playing down the significance of the situation
- Projection: Assigning negative qualities to others
- Rationalization: Making excuses for the situation through flawed reasoning
- Regression: Using former coping strategies that are inappropriate now (i.e., temper tantrums)
- Repression: Not accepting and expressing emotions
- Self-defeating behaviors: Sabotaging or procrastinating to avoid making progress
- Sublimation: Substituting more socially acceptable behaviors for unacceptable ones

Based on Connor 2005.

DEFENSE MECHANISM DETECTIVE'S LOG

As you read down the preceding list of defense mechanisms, look for them in politics, on the news, on reality shows. Looking for defense mechanisms in others may help you to see them in yourself.

START

Mindful sitting with journal

CUES

1. For a week, jot down instances of people using these mechanisms.
2. Reflect on when in the past you have used these same defense mechanisms. Reflect on your reactions to these defense mechanisms in others as well as in yourself. For example, you may scoff at a person who makes excuses for speeding, saying he had to get to work on time, and if he doesn't work, he can't feed his children, and then claims the officer is at fault for not caring about his children (rationalization). Now think back on what you might have rationalized your own speeding.

FINISH

Reflect on the circumstances in which you often use defense mechanisms (e.g., project deadlines). Can you use better coping skills rather than defense mechanisms? Make a sincere effort to notice how using defense mechanism puts up a shield to protect your ego or sense of self. What is the cost (e.g., offending or alienating friends)?

Summary

As you read this chapter on emotional wellness, did you feel resistant to using emotional stress management tools at any point? This raises the question of "secondary gains"—the benefits of staying stuck in difficult emotions (e.g., others taking on our responsibilities when we are sad and unable to cope). Staying stuck in negative emotions and not taking responsibility to process and deal with situations in health-enhancing ways can undermine our health. Being emotionally healthy is vital to wellness. Commit to practicing tools to boost your well-being including cultivating happiness, positivity, optimism, and empathy; laughing; doing music therapy; doing art therapy; and using multiple forms of intelligence.

Chapter 4 explores intellectual wellness and stress. It is difficult to distinguish between thinking (intellectual processes) and the emotions associated with thinking. The task is to be aware of how emotions influence our thinking and the subsequent actions we take, and to use stress management tools to regulate and express emotions in health-enhancing ways.

stress
chapter 4

Intellectual Wellness

I've always wanted to be able to see where my life would take me, and now I understand that I can, because I know there is a direct connection between what I say and what happens to me.

Jennifer Hudson

It is hard to discern whether our behaviors dictate our beliefs or our beliefs dictate our behaviors. Buddhist psychology lends an interesting perspective: your mind is just one of your sense organs; it is not who you are. The mind thinks just as the ear listens; thinking is just what it does.

Being aware of our perceptions, our cognitive interpretations of events, is the most critical aspect of stress management. Often it is not the event that causes the stress but our interpretation of it, and we have control of our interpretations. We may believe that someone has "made us feel bad" when actually the person has simply threatened our sense of well-being and comfort. The meaning given to situations determines the outcomes. Believing that we have power or control in the situation gives us a sense of empowerment instead of sending us into feelings of hopelessness and powerlessness.

One way we trigger stress is by ruminating—that is, continuing to think about an upsetting or unfair situation and being unwilling to let it go or move past it. We keep reliving the argument and thinking about how mad the other person made us. In this way we stew in the toxic environment of stress reactivity. This environment perpetuates the rehashing of the event, which creates a closed loop. As the cycle continues, the situation becomes even more awful and out of proportion, which is known as *awfulizing*.

Daniel Amen, in his book *Magnificent Mind at Any Age* (2008), suggested that our brains can be rewired to make healthier connections. This concept is called *neuroplasticity*, which is the brain's ability to stimulate new neural pathways and create new brain cells (*neurons*). These actions of the brain can result from activities such as those presented in this chapter, including meditation, creative imagination, and reframing.

We all have the capacity to change at any age. Negative thinking is a habit that causes the brain to overreact. We can improve the wiring to our prefrontal cortex to improve our critical thinking, creativity, and impulse control as well as to help us learn from previous experiences. This is especially important in the teen and young adult years because the prefrontal cortex is not fully developed until age 25. Unhealthy choices and habits can severely affect the development in this part of the brain. Amen's (2008) research on the best ways to protect our brains supports many of the suggestions presented in this textbook, including the following:

- Get enough sleep. This is important for the repair and growth of brain cells.
- Eat healthfully and stay hydrated. The brain uses 20 percent of the body's energy and requires large amounts of water to function.
- Be physically active. Physical activity increases blood flow to the brain and removes toxins.
- Avoid alcohol. Alcohol is a diuretic and depresses the brain's ability to learn and remember.

- Avoid nicotine. Nicotine decreases blood flow to the brain.
- Avoid excessive caffeine. Caffeine is a diuretic that interferes with restful sleep.

Addressing the intellectual dimension of wellness challenges us to keep our minds open and expand our perspective as much as possible. It is known that positive beliefs or intentions are concurrent with effective actions and success. By using the tools of mindfulness, problem solving, goal setting, disputation, imagination, and creativity, your perspective on stressful situations shifts from thinking of them as obstacles and problems to considering them challenges and maybe even opportunities and solutions. As Charles Rosner said, "If you're not part of the solution, you're part of the problem."

Mindfulness

Mindfulness-based stress reduction (MBSR) has played an important role in the field of stress management. Jon Kabat-Zinn, at the University of Massachusetts Medical Center in Worchester, Massachusetts, has been using MBSR with various population groups including adults and children for over 30 years. Vipassana meditation, an ancient form of mindfulness meditation presented here and used by Kabat-Zinn, means "seeing clearly"—in other words, seeing all aspects of who we are clearly.

Mindfulness is the act of paying attention on purpose to the present moment nonjudgmentally and with compassion and curiosity (Kabat-Zinn, 2009). According to Richard O'Connor (2005), mindfulness epitomizes the idea of being "cool" because it is about being detached and objective. Being cool is not about needing outside approval from others, but instead is about being self-assured with an internal locus of control. Mindfulness (i.e., choosing to be present) facilitates the shift to an internal locus of control. The opposite state would be called mindlessness—letting our thoughts rule by giving them more credit than warranted and chasing after them to wherever they may lead.

When we are mindful, we do not deny or shut off symptoms of stress. Rather, we sit with our experiences without attachment or judgment and ask, What is the message these mind–body signals are sending? Could the back pain I am feeling be a signal that I am carrying too much work and responsibility? Could the tiredness I am feeling be a message that I am doing too much and it is time to simplify and do less?

A major aspect of mindfulness is acceptance. We accept our body sensations, our thoughts, and our feelings; we sit with them and observe them without judging and getting involved in all the drama and stories associated with them. We can coexist with difficult feelings while at the same time setting goals and taking action toward

@ WEB LINK

Mindfulness

- Center for Mindfulness in Medicine, Health Care, and Society. This organization pioneered medical research in mindfulness-based stress reduction. www.umassmed.edu/content.aspx?id=41252
- UCLA Mindful Awareness Research Center (MARC). This website has a lot of information and research on mindfulness. http://marc.ucla.edu
- MARC also offers free meditation podcasts. http://marc.ucla.edu/body.cfm?id=22

what is important. Mindfulness means resisting the tendency to allow our energy to be carried away by unproductive and habitual thoughts such as *I am stupid* or *No one likes me*. Such thoughts take away from our quality of life right now.

When we practice mindfulness, we manage stress by letting unproductive emotions and thoughts go and enjoying the present. Stress can be viewed as a reaction to the past or a projection into the future—both of which are out of our locus of control. Mindfulness helps us choose being fully present and attending to what is here right now over stress reactivity.

Practicing mindfulness, or focused concentration, is a lot like training a puppy. The key is not to chastise or scold yourself when you feel distracted, but to return to the present with kindness, compassion, and patience. It is just a habit for the mind to run off and not focus. This is normal! Practicing mindfulness helps to turn off the stress response by preventing sensory overload and also unclutters the mind. We pay attention to what is here now and within our power. This does not mean that we do not plan for the future; we simply do so in a mindful way: curious, open, and nonjudgmental.

You may find that sitting quietly is a habit you are not used to. An important part of mindfulness is paying attention to the sensations that arise. We want to be open to it all—not try to stop our thoughts, sensations, and emotions but become aware of them without attaching to them or judging them.

Following are the qualities of mindfulness:

- Being objective and nonjudgmental
- Acknowledging everything
- Not striving
- Having self-compassion

Be mindful by living in the moment instead of dwelling on the past or worrying about the future. Experience the moment you are in right now.

- Observing the present from moment to moment
- Letting be and allowing
- Being self-reliant
- Being awake

There are many ways to bring mindfulness into your everyday life. The following list provides some examples.

- Before jumping out of bed, take five minutes to be quiet and still. You can meditate, read inspirational passages, stay quiet, or stretch.
- When in your car—at a traffic light, waiting for the car to warm up—come into mindful breathing.
- During your normal stances (standing, seated, lying down), notice whether your body is holding tension. Are your hands gripping the steering wheel? Are your shoulders hunched over your laptop? Is your jaw clenched when you are falling asleep?
- Turn off your normal distractions (car radio while driving, TV while eating, phone while studying).
- Honor the transitions during your day. Instead of rushing from your room to your first class, take time to pause; take a few breaths.
- Take breaks mindfully. Eat lunch at a table rather than at your work desk; take a walk instead of drinking coffee, stuffing down a snack, or having a cigarette.
- Set up your day for mindfulness, with reminders to stop, find your breath, and be still for a few moments. Put an alarm on your phone to ring every hour; do this every time you sit down at your desk, or before making a phone call.
- Have a silent meal without reading the newspaper or watching TV.
- Find mini mindful moments: walking to your car, driving, doing laundry, taking a shower, washing dishes, downloading onto your computer, waiting on hold.
- Practice being mindful when communicating. Use active listening and mindful speaking.
- Behave like a child. When you were a young child, you played games and invented new worlds without a lot of judgment or censorship—you just enjoyed them. You approached things with what is called a beginner's mind.

MINDFUL BREATHING REMINDERS

Write down some times in your day when you could practice being mindful—at school, work, or home, and during regular activities such as brushing your teeth or walking to class. Set up ways to remind yourself to practice mindfulness (e.g., an alarm on your phone, sticky notes).

WALKING MEDITATION

This activity uses walking as a focus.

START

Find a safe place to walk—a trail or open space such as a lawn or an indoor space. A hallway about 10 to 15 feet (3 to 4.6 m) long is ideal. It is nice to do this activity in bare feet to really feel the contact with the earth or floor.

CUES

1. Take 10 slow, deliberate steps as if you were moving in slow motion. Walk as slowly as you can and exaggerate picking up each foot and placing it on the floor or ground in front of you. Pay attention to all the aspects of walking by bringing your complete focus on the movement of your arms; your torso, legs, and feet; and your breath.

2. Continue to walk with mindfulness. If you become distracted, stop and take a deep breath and continue your slow walking.

FINISH

Standing still, close your eyes and take three deep, relaxing breaths.

OUTDOOR WALKING MEDITATION

This activity focuses on the sounds, smells, and colors of the outdoors.

START

Find a place outdoors where you can safely practice mindful walking.

CUES

As you walk mindfully outdoors, focus on the following:

- How many smells can you notice?
- How many shapes and colors?
- How many sounds?
- How many sights?
- What textures do you feel?

FINISH

Take a moment to reflect on how it feels to pay attention to nature as a stress management tool.

MINDFULNESS-BASED MEDITATION

This activity focuses on the breath, the body, sound, emotion, and thoughts. The script allows for the slow building of a mindful meditation practice. The meditation is flexible in that you can choose to focus on any of the following:

- One area
- Each area in succession
- Whatever area shows up in your awareness

START

Mindful sitting

CUES

1. *Breath focus.* Bring your focus to your breath without changing it. Just observe your breath wherever it shows up. Make a deliberate intention to connect to your breath. Pay attention to all the sensations of your natural breath. Keep this focus as long as you wish.

2. *Sound focus.* Bring your focus to any sounds you might hear, and name them. Listen for external and internal noises such as your breath. Continue to listen without starting an internal dialogue; simply name the sound and then be quiet until the next sound comes to your attention. Stay with this focus as long as you wish.

3. *Body focus.* Bring your focus to your body. Notice any sensations you are having. Acknowledge each sensation by naming it, but do not allow an internal dialogue or story to begin. Stay with this focus as long as you wish.

4. *Emotion focus.* Bring your focus to any emotions you may be feeling. Name each one; if you do not know what you are feeling, keep it simple with just a word such as *discomfort* or *confusion*. Bring awareness but do not engage in an internal dialogue. Stay with this focus as long as you wish.

5. *Thought focus.* Witness any thoughts you are having right now. When a thought comes, label it as simply as possible (e.g., *thinking, planning*). Allow the thought to dissipate by not giving it energy or creating a story about it.

6. *Flexible focus.* Focus on whatever area shows up by staying present and curious to whatever comes along without being carried away. Just observe without judgment or attachment.

7. Now imagine that you are at the beach watching the waves ebb and flow. Just like waves, allow your breath, sounds, bodily sensations, thoughts, and emotions come in and float away. Just let them ebb and flow; they show up and they leave. Witness the constant changing without getting caught up in the ebb and flow. Observe the ebb and flow without analyzing or controlling, just with awareness.

8. Listen to the sound of your breath as you slowly fall into a deep silence, with only the sound of your breath ebbing and flowing softly and quietly. As your outer body softens, feel your inner body brighten. Smile with your heart as you dissolve, melt, let go, or toss aside any lingering tension, tightness, or aches.

FINISH

Take a few deep breaths and slowly let go of your meditation practice. Congratulate yourself on taking the time to practice mindfulness.

EATING A RAISIN

This activity develops mindfulness through various senses. It is also an important exercise for building awareness about mindful eating—taking the time to taste, chew, and experience our food.

MATERIALS

Several raisins or pieces of crackers or another food of your choice

START

Mindful sitting

CUES

1. In this activity, you pay attention to all of your senses when eating. Try not to go into judgment about your preferences and memories about the food you are eating; just focus on mindful eating.

2. Pick up the raisin (or cracker or whatever food you have chosen) and look at it. Notice its color, shape, texture, and weight. Explore it as much as possible with your eyes and fingers.

3. Spend some time smelling the food and then place it between your lips. Do not bite it yet. Feel the texture of it.

4. Allow the food to fall onto your tongue and, without biting, taste it. Move it around to different parts of your tongue. Bite down and chew it with as many bites as possible before you swallow it. Count how many bites you can complete before you swallow.

5. Notice how your mouth feels once the food is swallowed. Notice the aftertaste. Take a few moments to sit quietly.

6. You can repeat these steps with a new piece of food.

FINISH

Reflect on what it was it like to eat more slowly and with attention.

MY MIND CLOCK

In this activity you explore how much time you spend being mindful.

START

Mindful sitting with journal

CUES

1. Draw a large circle. Divide this circle into percentages of how much of your day your mind is on various activities: commuting, eating, working, studying, talking to friends.

2. Within each percentage, color with a darker color the amount of that time you spend mindfully (fully present).

3. Reflect on how much of your time you are distracted, busy, or paying attention to things outside of yourself.

FINISH

Set a goal to be more mindful in one area of your life that warrants it.

@ WEB LINK AND RESOURCE

Mindful Eating

- Albers, S. (2006). *Mindful eating 101: A guide to healthy eating in college and beyond*. New York: Routledge Taylor Francis Group.

- Eating Mindfully is a website provided by Dr. Susan Albers, a psychologist at the Cleveland Clinic, who has extensive experience working with college students and mindful eating. This website contains great tools to show you how to practice mindful eating. http://eatingmindfully.com/mindful-eating-tools/

Meditation

The word *meditation* can conjure up images of sitting cross-legged and making strange noises. It might be helpful to think of meditation as just a way to come into focused concentration. Meditation can be a lifelong skill that can enhance our ability to pay attention and concentrate.

Many have the misunderstanding that meditation is synonymous with thought stopping or coming into a trance, or zombie-like state. However, in meditation we are fully awake. Thoughts may be ubiquitous, but they are transient. We can consciously choose not to follow every one of them. Meditation asks us to become aware of thoughts—*Huh, I am thinking again*—and then to use this awareness to gently come back to whatever point of focus you've selected, such as your breath. The awareness of thoughts is part of the meditation process; they should not be something we fight or try to stop having. We can put them gently aside and come back to the choice to remain focused.

Research on the benefits of meditation is revealing it to be a strong tool anyone can use to become more focused, alert, mindful, creative, and relaxed. Research has shown that meditation not only decreases stress but also increases feelings of well-being and even happiness. People who have practiced long-term meditation have been found to have changes in the part of the brain—the prefrontal cortex—associated with happiness and wellness (Lazar et al., 2005). Meditation is associated with alpha waves, which are slow with low amplitude. Alpha waves create a restful state with associated health benefits, including decreasing headaches, blood pressure, and pain.

In his timeless book *The Relaxation Response* (2000), Benson suggested that the following components are essential for practicing meditation: a relaxed position in a quiet area, a mental focus tool, and an attitude of not striving or forcing. Benson recommended "passive concentration" when practicing meditation as well as relaxation. This means paying attention without judging the experience. He found that his patients were often not sure they were doing a "good job" at meditation. However, when he studied his patients while they were practicing meditation, he

Meditating is as simple as allowing yourself to relax and the mind to rest. Imagine all of the things troubling you washing away.

discovered that they had lowered heart and breathing rates and oxygen consumption whether they believed that they were practicing correctly or not.

Here are some guidelines for meditation practice:

- Practice several forms of meditation until you find one that works. If you are a strongly kinesthetic learner (i.e., you learn best through movement), then consider doing a walking meditation or yoga. If you are an auditory learner, using a mantra as a source of focus might be a good choice.

- Use sound as the focus of your meditation. In his book *Meditation for Beginners*, Jack Kornfield, a renowned scholar in meditation, explained that when we focus on sounds within and around us, "we open the meditation to all the music of life, to the dance of the energies we experience when we sit. We use the breath in the center of it as a way to still ourselves and become peaceful, and then we use that awareness to meet whatever arises with kindness and acceptance" (2008, p. 55).

- Be patient with all emotions that come forth. A wise rule is this: If it's good, don't attach to it; if it's bad, don't run away.

- Use a dhristi, or point of focus, as an anchor. This could be specific aspect of your breath (e.g., focusing on when your breath enters your nostrils), a candle, a symbol such as artwork, an aspect of nature such as a pebble, or a talisman (an object you can hold in your hands that has special meaning for you). Some people use rosary beads.

- Imagine your emotions or thoughts projected on a large-screen TV. Allow the image of these thoughts to come and go without judging them, making up a drama about them, or filtering them; just observe them.

- Acknowledge that you will be distracted. Our society is full of distractions, and meditation helps us to focus and do one thing. If persistent thoughts come to mind, notice them and let them go. The image of a brook or stream with leaves or twigs can help; imagine that your thoughts are like leaves and twigs on the surface of the water. Notice them and let them float on by.

- When you catch yourself thinking, just return to your anchor without a lot of fuss. This is a necessary part of meditation: noticing when you wander away from your focus and gently coming back.

- Set an intention to give a thought your attention at a later time—for now you are meditating. When thoughts demand your attention, just graciously say "later" or "drop the call." If they are important, you can attend to them later.

- Witness your thoughts by *naming* them with words such as *thinking, planning,* or *remembering*—to keep it simple. Kornfield (2008) identified this naming as "an aid to help us simply be aware of whatever is happening. You can use what serves you, and if it does not, you can just let your awareness be with whatever is present" (p. 55).

@ WEB LINK

Meditation

The National Center for Complementary and Alternative Medicine. This center within the U.S. National Institutes of Health offers a large amount of research on meditation. http://nccam.nih.gov/health/meditation

FOCUS on Research

Mindfulness Investigation

Lazar and colleagues (2005) compared brain activity in experienced meditators with that in novice meditators (16 participants in each group). Brain activity was measured during meditation, at rest, and in response to sounds designed to evoke emotional responses: a negative sound (a woman in distress), a positive sound (a baby laughing), and a neutral sound (a busy restaurant). The researchers found that both groups of meditators showed an increased empathetic reaction while meditating. The expert meditators showed a much greater reaction, especially to the negative sound, which may point to an increased capacity for empathy as a result of their extensive meditation training.

- Be a rookie. Many meditation teachers tout the importance of having a "beginner's mind." Instead of automatically judging or assuming things about your practice, just show up with an open attitude. Ask yourself: *What can I learn here about myself?* Expectations distract us from just letting things happen.

- Make a commitment to and set time aside for meditation. For each of the meditation activities in this chapter, use a timer. The ritual of setting a timer reinforces your intention to commit to the activity. Research has revealed that the most significant changes were found in long-term meditators who practiced 45 minutes or an hour every day. This may seem overwhelming, but keep in mind that the important concept is practice. Consider doing 10 minutes per day in a formal activity and perhaps two or three breaks during the day in which you practice for one or two minutes.

- When walking or running, focus on your foot strike on the pavement or the sensations in your muscles. Walking is often used as a moving meditation with a focus on the mechanics of the heel lift, the transfer of weight to the front of the foot, the shifting of weight, and the push-off from the toes. Young children practice mindful walking when learning to walk; their entire focus is on placing one foot in front of the other.

- Sit upright without straining but as strong and tall as you comfortably can. Lying down can encourage falling asleep.

- Give yourself permission to modify any of the cues or suggestions to make them work for you. If you feel uncomfortable closing your eyes, just soften your eye gaze a few feet (a meter or so) in front of you.

CHOOSING A MANTRA

A form of meditation called transcendental meditation (TM) uses a mantra, which is a simple word, sound, or sentence repeated over and over as the focus of attention, or anchor. In TM, a spiritual teacher, or guru, assigns the mantra to the student. In this activity, you choose your own power word or words. A mantra is one word, several words, a short sentence, or a sound that is of special significance, such as *peace, shalom, I am powerful, om*. The sound of *om* is done as follows: On the inhale, make the sound of *ahhh* (the sound of a relaxed sigh); on the exhale, make the sound of *ommm* (the sound of contentment).

Here is an example of a simple mantra by Thich Nhat Hahn: *Breathing in I am calm; breathing out I smile.*

START

Mindful sitting with a timer. Set the timer for whatever time you have chosen to dedicate to this meditation activity.

CUES

1. Choose your own simple mantra.
2. Once you have chosen your mantra, come into slow, relaxed breathing.
3. Start to repeat your mantra slowly to yourself on each breath cycle.
4. Set the intention to let go of any thoughts or distractions. Come back to your mantra and inner peace and calm.

FINISH

Reflect on how using a mantra affected your meditation practice.

Changing Distorted Thinking, Reframing, and Disputation

A strengths-based approach to stress management focuses on a healthy and truthful sense of self. When we skillfully apply strength-based stress management tools, we are whole, present right here and right now, and not fragmented. Being still and quiet is often interrupted by the constant stream of dialogue that goes on in our minds.

A great deal of this dialogue is negative, which is why I call it *negative self-talk.* These negative statements may reflect comments made to us in our past by family members, peers, and teachers that have become woven into our own stream of thoughts. Self-talk is when we filter all thinking and feelings through a continuous feedback loop. When we are under stress, our perception tends to be negative and can bring on irrational thoughts that fuel this continuous loop of self-loathing and animosity. Notice how many times you use the phrases *I can't, I never, I don't,* or *I should.* When we repeat these often enough, we come to believe that they are true, when in fact they are not. This sets us up for a self-fulfilling prophecy of failure and pessimism. Our negative self-talk is self-centered and judgmental and focuses on the drama of our deficiencies. Three methods for changing negative self-talk into positive self-talk are changing distorted thinking, reframing, and disputation. Positive self-talk allows us to stop focusing on negative thoughts when we are faced with challenges and develops into an important skill for enhancing our wellness.

Changing Distorted Thinking

Our thoughts can easily be blown out of proportion and become distorted. Thought distortions are irrational ways of thinking or beliefs we have that interfere with our ability to think positively or realistically about situations. Distorted thinking is sometimes referred to as *mind traps* and can become a habit. We feel justified in prolonging our negative thoughts.

The first step in dealing with this constant judging and critical chatter is to become aware of it. Often, just paying attention to how warped or biased the statements are is an eye-opener. Notice that these statements can become worse when we are not at our best—when we are sleep deprived, dehydrated, or running on empty. In the book *The Feeling Good Handbook*, David Burns (1999) identified self-limiting thoughts and destructive beliefs that interfere with our ability to think health-enhancing thoughts (see table 4.1).

TABLE 4.1   Examples of Switching From Distorted Thinking to Realistic Thinking

Thought distortion	Example of distorted thinking	Switching to realistic thinking
Self-blame Taking everything personally by blaming yourself for the event or assuming that because you feel a certain way, you are responsible.	Because I forgot I had planned to work out with some friends at the fitness center, I'm a bad person.	Making a mistake is unfortunate, but it does not mean I am a bad person.
Mental filter Dwelling on negatives.	Person A was mean to me. Nobody likes me.	Person A was mean to me, but there are many people who like me.
Overgeneralization Overexaggerating: one situation is seen as the norm; it will always be this way.	I am physically out of shape and will always be this way.	I can implement a plan to improve my physical fitness.
Black-or-white thinking Thinking in absolutes as if the situation is all or nothing; it is one way or the other and there is no middle ground or shades of gray.	My life is empty and worthless now that my girlfriend/boyfriend has dumped me.	My lost love does not constitute my whole life.
It's all about me Having a sense of entitlement. Things should or must happen according to your agenda, or you play the victim and assert that things are never your fault.	My professor is mad at me because I scored low on the test.	The professor is frustrated because the class as a whole scored low on the test.
It all sucks Blowing situations out of proportion, making negative conclusions without facts, or spinning a constant pessimistic twist. Seeing the worst in situations (i.e., "awfulizing").	I binged on cookies today and didn't follow my daily healthy eating plan. I will never lose weight.	One day of not following my eating plan does not mean I have failed in my nutrition program. I can and will lose weight.
Musts Putting limitations or unrealistic attachments on situations. Knowing better than everyone. Perfectionist thinking using words such as *should* and *always*.	I must get an A or I will flunk out of school.	I will graduate, and less than an A will not stop me.
Jumping to conclusions and making assumptions without proof.	Guys just dump me without giving the relationship a chance.	Not all guys act this way. I need to be patient and give the next guy a chance.

Adapted from Burns 1999.

Reframing

When faced with challenging situations, especially when we are angry or scared, we have a tendency to have tunnel vision. A better plan is to widen our focus—to think outside the box and see the big picture. Reframing, also known as cognitive restructuring, is the practice of changing our perspective of a situation. When we adopt an attitude of self-responsibility, we own what is true and kick to the curb defeating and negative beliefs (Burns, 1999).

Tips for Reframing

- Try to find a positive explanation for the situation.
- Put the situation in perspective. How can you view it in a more holistic and healthier way? Try to change the framing of your words and use less dramatic or emotionally packed language to describe the situation.
- If you are not part of the solution, the problem remains a problem. What action could you take instead of dwelling on the problem, "chewing and stewing," and perpetuating the stress cycle? Set an intention of not allowing any disturbing thoughts to override the best response to the situation.

So much of our thoughts are not supportive of our health and happiness. If you took the time to really listen to the constant stream of stinking thinking you do every day, you may be surprised at how automatic it is to be punitive and downright mean to yourself.

Disputation

Disputation is the process of putting thoughts logically and rationally to the test to see whether there is any evidence that they are true. Disputation is the opposite of distortion, and it is critical for changing to a more optimistic viewpoint.

Albert Ellis, a psychologist, developed rational emotive behavior therapy to investigate irrational beliefs and unrealistic expectations (2001). He created the ABCDE formula to help people investigate their beliefs and expectations—to dispute them or put them to the test. Disputation asks us to bring awareness to our reactive judgments and habitual thinking. Instead of indulging automatic statements such as *I always* or *I never*, we can put these thoughts to a test to see whether they are true.

Here are some disputation tools:

- Adopt a more positive explanation of what is happening. Can you spin your beliefs into a more realistic point of view?
- Acknowledge that your thoughts are correct, but rather than stew in them, look for a solution to the problem you are facing.
- Think about just how important this problem is in the scheme of things. In the bigger picture of your day, week, or month, how important is this problem?

@ WEB LINK

Changing Distorted Thinking, Reframing, and Disputation

Center for Investigating Healthy Minds. This center located at the University of Wisconsin at Madison conducts scientific research to increase knowledge about ways to nourish positive qualities of mind. www.investigatinghealthyminds.org

Ellis' ABCDE Formula

- **A** = **A**ctivating event or situation. Example: *I flunked a quiz.*
- **B** = **B**eliefs. Example: *The instructor is out to get me. I hate this class; what a waste of time. I am lazy and unmotivated.*
- **C** = **C**onsequences. How you react to the activating event. Example: *I'll stop going to class. I feel discouraged and ready to withdraw from this class. It is pointless to try to catch up now.*
- **D** = **D**isputation. Many times our beliefs are based on irrational, automatic, negative thoughts; these can shift to rational thoughts.
- **E** = **E**vidence. Look at the evidence, or facts, to support your stressful thoughts. "Thinking traps" occur when assumptions are made without relevant information.

To find about more about Ellis' work, see the website for the Albert Ellis Institute and Rational Emotional Behavior Technique at www.rebt.org/public/about-rebt.html.

REBT Self-help Form. New York: Albert Ellis Institute, 2009.

If you find yourself still stuck, can you find a way to distract yourself or find a positive thing you can do to just let go of the negativity, such as take a walk, journal, or talk it out with someone you trust and who can provide some honest feedback?

JOURNALING ABOUT A DISTRESSING THOUGHT AND REFRAMING

This activity offers steps to consider when using reframing.

START

Mindful sitting with journal

CUES

1. Identify a stressful situation you have experienced and what you were feeling at the time.
2. What thoughts did you have during the situation? Was there a particularly distressing thought?
3. Take this distressing thought and consider a more balanced view of the situation with a more open and objective perspective. Ask yourself this question: *How can I reframe this situation?*
4. If you are uncertain about how to reframe the situation, take more time to examine it or ask someone for help.
5. If you confront a situation like this again, what actions might you take (including no action)? Write an affirmation affirming a positive outlook.

FINISH

How can reframing help you leave your myopic lens and look at situations from a broader perspective?

STOPPING NEGATIVE SELF-TALK: STOP, DROP, AND BREATHE

Thought stopping is the deliberate practice of stopping negative self-talk by bringing the focus back to a focus device such as breaths in the belly, and replacing these thoughts with calming statements. This activity uses the image of a traffic light as a visual reminder to stop (red light), slow down (yellow light), and give the green light to positive thoughts. You can use this image whenever you feel overwhelmed by negative thoughts.

START

Mindful sitting

CUES

1. Take a moment to think about a particular concern or worry you are experiencing.
2. Picture a traffic light. Focus your attention on the red circle and say to yourself, *STOP.* Do this as many times as necessary to stop the thoughts.
3. Now shift your focus to the yellow circle of the traffic light. Drop your hands to your lower abdomen and take deep diaphragmatic breaths into your belly and say to yourself, *Slow down.* Do this as often as needed until your breathing is relaxed and calm.
4. As you now shift your focus to the green circle, reword and use a positive statement to replace the negative thoughts, such as *I can handle this* or *I am OK right now*. Repeat this affirming statement as often as needed until you feel calm and centered.

FINISH

Take a few moments to reflect on how you feel now. Consider situations in which you could use this technique, such as before exams. Set an intention to practice this technique in your life.

OBSERVING SELF-TALK

In this activity you take time to look at your habitual self-talk in a calm and relaxing atmosphere.

START

Mindful sitting with journal

CUES

1. Take a few moments to slow down your breath so you become calm and relaxed. Set an intention to take an honest look at your self-talk.
2. Write down as many typical self-talk statements you can think of. Notice the feelings that arise when you think of these statements.
3. To shift to an internal locus of control to have a positive perspective, state silently, *It is OK to have my _____ feelings. My feelings don't need to control my behavior.*

4. Say to yourself: *I will* _____ [state an action that reflects an internal locus of control].

FINISH

Set up reminders to practice restating self-talk several times a day. Notice when you start to go into automatic negative language and the emotional states that set this off.

WHAT IF?

We often fall into a deep well of "awfulizing." We allow ourselves to imagine all the awful "what ifs" or worst-case scenarios. What if you did the opposite? In this activity, imagine what would happen if you could see the situation in a positive light.

START

Mindful sitting

CUES

1. Practice deep, relaxing breathing for a few minutes until you feel centered and grounded and ready to do this activity.
2. Think about a situation that is causing you worry. Make a sincere effort to say (and believe) the following: *What if a better outcome happened here?* Allow yourself to creatively imagine a better outcome.
3. If your worry persists, resist the inner critic and bring your focus back to the question: *What if a better outcome happened here?*
4. Take as long as you need to fully explore your creative response to this question.

FINISH

Take a few deep breaths when you are finished. Are there any actions you want to take in response to the "What if?" exercise?

CHANGE YOUR LIFE; CHANGE YOUR MIND

This activity helps you recognize stressful thoughts and shift to a positive outlook.

START

Mindful sitting

CUES

1. Take a few deep, relaxing breaths to feel as comfortable as possible and come into a state of calm and focus. Take as long as necessary to become calm and focused.
2. Bring into your awareness a difficult thought you are experiencing right now.
3. Replace this thought with a more positive one. Use a short statement that reflects your decision to change your mind. Repeat this as often as necessary.

FINISH

Reflect on how you might use this technique in your life. In what situations would it be helpful?

SHIFTING THE LOCUS OF CONTROL

In this activity you list the typical internal statements you make that are focused on an external locus of control—placing blame, responsibility, or power on things outside of yourself. You take each statement and shift to an internal locus of control.

START

Mindful sitting with journal

CUES

1. Write as many statements as you can that focus on placing blame on others or giving control to others or situations.
2. Now rewrite each statement, shifting to an internal locus of control that focuses on your choices and your responsibilities. For examples, see table 4.2.

TABLE 4.2   Shifting the Locus of Control

External locus of control	Internal locus of control
I am not good at math. The instructors at this school are so useless. I'll never be good at math.	I need to pass math and will take the time to study and get a tutor to help me.
That person is so rude, and she drives me crazy.	That person's attitude is poor, but I can take steps to get away from her or not react to her taunts.

FINISH

Take time during your day to notice negative, external locus of control thinking, and shift to positive, internal locus of control thinking.

PROCESSING USING THOUGHT STOPPING

This activity provides a systematic way to process negative thinking situations using the ABCDE formula.

START

Mindful sitting with journal using Ellis' ABCDE formula

CUES

1. Describe a problem or recent situation that you are concerned about (A = activating event). Include the emotions and feelings you experience when faced with this situation. Try to capture the situation as completely as possible.
2. List the automatic thoughts that you have about this events (B = beliefs). Identify your distorted thinking about this situation.
3. What actions did you take (C = consequences) as a result of A and B?
4. Take each belief you listed in step 2 and use the questions in step 5 to put it to the test (D = disputation).

5. What rationale (E = evidence) do you have to support this belief? Ask the following questions:

    • What is false or exaggerated about this belief? What judgments and expectations does it reflect, of yourself or others?

    • What is the worst thing that could happen if this belief were true?

    • What might be some good things about this situation?

    • What would happen if you eased up a bit on your judgment in this situation?

Based on Ellis 2001.

FINISH

Reflect on what you have learned about using the tool of disputation. How do you feel after completing this exercise? How might you deal with these thoughts in the future?

Affirmations

Affirmations are powerful, succinct statements of things we want to have happen in our lives. We repeat them to remind us of our capacity to change negative thinking to positive thinking. In affirmations, we match what we want with actions we can take to get it.

Commercials depend on our remembering slogans so we later purchase the products. Athletes and businesspeople use affirmations to help them achieve goals and success. It may feel awkward to use these statements, but with practice and

What do you want to happen in your life? Say it out loud in an affirmation and imagine how great you will feel when you achieve your goals!

patience, they may begin to feel more natural, and your new beliefs will create a new experience.

Keep the following in mind when writing affirmations:

- Depending on your preferred learning style, use any of the following:
    - Visual: Use imagery along with words.
    - Auditory: Repeat the statements aloud over and over.
    - Kinesthetic: Repeat the statements in rhythm with your movement while walking or working out.
- Keep your statements in the present tense.
- Use positive language; don't use *I won't* or *no* in your statements.
- Make a sincere effort to believe in your statement. Sometimes you have to "fake it 'til you make it." This means to act as if this statement has been manifested and allow yourself to feel what it would be like to realize this statement.
- Make your statements meaningful and personal.
- Keep your wording specific, simple, and succinct.
- Use words that capture how you will feel when you have achieved your goal: *I did it!*
- Repeat often!

WRITING AFFIRMATIONS

This activity provides practice in using affirmations.

START

Mindful sitting with journal or index cards

CUES

1. Use one or more of the following starts to affirmations that you will write in your journal or on index cards: *I am* _____ [something about your character; e.g., *I am motivated*]; *I can* _____ [something about your potential; e.g., *I can set goals and achieve them*]; *I will* _____ [what you sincerely want to have happen; e.g., *I will get into graduate school*].

2. Take a deep inhale and softly state your affirmations aloud on the exhale. With each subsequent exhale, say the affirmation a little more quietly until you are saying it silently to yourself.

3. Pay attention to each word you say, and don't rush. All the words in the affirmation matter, so take the time to say them with purpose and intention.

4. Feel the words you have selected intuitively; go beyond the words until you have a sense of the spirit behind them.

5. Take a few letting-go breaths, and on your exhales, continue to say your affirmations silently.

FINISH

Schedule several times during your day to sit quietly and recite your affirmations. As you plan your day, restate your affirmations so you can commit your energy and time to receiving what you want in your heart of hearts.

I COULD CHOOSE

This affirmation activity uses statements about qualities you want to encourage in your life.

START

Mindful sitting with journal or index cards

CUES

1. Consider a stressful situation you are experiencing right now or that happened recently.
2. Write an affirmation that identifies your reaction to the situation and how you might respond instead. Example: *Instead of _____* [e.g., giving up], *I could choose _____* [e.g., patience].
3. Write your affirmation on an index card, as a journal entry, or as an electronic reminder.
4. Close your eyes and repeat the statement as often as needed to feel the words permeate and take hold.
5. Repeat this activity several times daily.

You can extend this affirmation activity as a journal activity. Spend some time reflecting on how you can use this affirmation as a stress management tool.

FINISH

Take a few letting-go breaths as you finish this activity. Notice how you feel.

AFFIRMATIONS OF APPRECIATION

This activity helps you appreciate even difficult times.

START

Mindful sitting with journal or index cards

CUES

Use the following sentences to start off your affirmations:

- *I am lucky to _____.*
- *I am grateful for _____.*
- *My best friend _____.*
- *Today was _____; I know tomorrow will be better. I am choosing to bring _____ to myself right now.*

FINISH

Take a few letting-go breaths as you finish this activity. Notice how you feel.

Use a journal to list your goals and come up with a plan to reach them.

Goal Setting and Problem Solving

Many of us take failure badly and give up. Instead of viewing failure as an end point, however, we can choose to learn from the setback to focus on actions needed for reaching our goals. The process of working toward goals is actually more important than achieving those goals. For example, you may never win a marathon, but establishing a workout plan, disciplining yourself to go for a run rather than sleep in, and making a contract with a running partner are all part of a skill set you can use many times over to stay in shape and feel healthy.

One problem with focusing on outcomes is that it keeps us from changing long-term behaviors that caused the problem in the first place. We may lose weight on a strict diet or by using diet pills, but avoid addressing long-term behaviors such as eating smaller portions and exercising 30 minutes a day. Without making such changes part of our lifestyles, we will probably fail at keeping the weight off in the long run.

Tips for Following Through With Goals

- Keep in mind that practice makes perfect.
- Find support, someone to talk with about your goal or to buddy up with.
- Take baby steps. Set yourself up to build on your success with regular, small gains rather than going overboard, burning out, and giving up.
- Make the process enjoyable.
- Be determined; set your mind to it. Change is not easy, but with discipline and grace, you can do it.
- Be real; ask yourself whether this is your goal or imposed by someone else.
- Adjust your attitude toward your goals.

- Make your goals holistic, not just about one area of your life (e.g., school). Set goals that will enhance your emotional well-being (socializing with friends, volunteering); create a balance that is challenging but meaningful for you.
- Prepare. Have a plan B and a plan C.
- Regroup, learn from setbacks, and keep reworking your action steps.
- Reward yourself! You will be more likely to sustain your success by rewarding your consistent small gains.

STEPS TO SETTING A GOAL JOURNAL ACTIVITY

This activity offers a structure for planning goals.

START

Writing goals down is the best way to be committed to and accountable for your goals.

CUES

1. Make your goal as specific as possible (e.g., *I will earn an A in my biology class*).
2. Determine how you will measure (keep a record of) your progress toward your goal (e.g., *I will receive a 90 percent or higher on my weekly biology lab report, quizzes, and assigned papers*). Devise a way to chart your progress.
3. List the specific actions you will take to achieve this goal. This is where you might need to map out the semester and keep a checklist of specific tasks (actions) you must complete. These tasks might be reading chapters, making flash cards, reviewing notes with a study group, and attending labs.
4. For each task in step 3, assign a deadline. Devise a way to keep track of these deadlines.
5. Review your progress toward your goal weekly, checking each of the previous steps. Reflect on any of the steps you were not able to complete and consider things you could do to make these easier.

FINISH

Reflect on how creating accountability has helped you move toward meeting your goal. It is also critical to reflect on what did not work and find ways to adapt the goal to make it work for you. Don't give up the goal entirely, but deliberate ways to be successful. You might find it useful to team up with a friend and meet weekly to share your progress toward your goals. Help each other determine where you had difficulties and troubleshoot ways to make progress.

HOW I SET MYSELF UP NOT TO MEET MY GOALS

This journal activity can help you examine how you process goals, including ways you sabotage or interfere with following through with your intentions. If you find that you are not making progress toward a goal, this activity will help you take an honest look at how and why you are not achieving your goal.

START

Mindful sitting with journal

CUES

1. Take a few deep breaths and set an intention to take an honest look at your goal-setting patterns.
2. Think about a goal you set in the past and had every intention of accomplishing, but did not.
3. Write this goal as specifically as you can remember it.
4. Consider the following about your goal:
   - How realistic was your goal?
   - How personal was this goal? What motivated you to select this goal?
   - How prepared were you to take action to achieve this goal?
   - Did your intentions match your commitment to this goal?
   - How much support did you seek for achieving this goal?
   - What barriers did you face in pursuing this goal, and what did you do to combat them?
   - Did you procrastinate or become negative about your ability to achieve this goal?
   - Did you take the time to plan for meeting this goal? What information did you need but did not get?
   - Did you set up a system of accountability and objectivity regarding this goal (e.g., a spreadsheet with clear goals such as number of portions eaten or amount of time studying)?
   - Was your goal concrete (i.e., measurable) or vague? Was your accountability system simple or too complicated or cumbersome?

FINISH

What have you learned about yourself and setting goals? What are some ways you can use this information when setting goals in the future?

MONEY MANAGEMENT: WHAT I SPEND MY MONEY ON

Concerns about money are one of the leading sources of stress among millennials (American Psychological Association, 2012). This activity will help you objectively and truthfully look at how you spend your money and consider ways to better manage money.

CUES

1. Find a method to keep track of your spending (e.g., your phone, a spreadsheet, a written log). Commit to being diligent about recording every dime you spend.
2. After a period of time (e.g., a week or a month), reflect on your patterns of spending. On what areas do you overspend? Do you buy things you don't need or make decisions about money without thinking them through (e.g., buying rounds of drinks)?

3. Set a budget. Bring only the amount of money you have delegated to spend in a particular situation (e.g., eating out with friends).

4. Avoid "one-click" impulse buying online (meaning you do not have to put in information—the computer already knows your credit card!). Wait a day before buying something to make sure you are not buying on impulse, using online shopping as a form of procrastination or task avoidance, or wanting to win out on a bid (e.g., an eBay auction).

5. Adopt the mantra: Reuse, reduce, recycle. Have a recycling party; invite people to bring clothes or other items that don't fit or no longer work for them but are in good condition, and initiate trades.

FINISH

What do you now know about how you spend money and when and where you may be spending unnecessarily? You may notice that you are shopping to feel better, and you may recognize that there are ways to feel better without shopping. Also consider where you might be wasting money such as buying lunch every day at a fast-food place instead of using your dining hall or packing a lunch.

CREATIVE PROBLEM SOLVING

This activity will help you consider a problem you are having trouble resolving.

START

Mindful sitting with journal. Take a few deep, relaxing breaths. Practice alternate nostril breathing or wake-up breath (both described in chapter 2). These activities will help your brain come into a relaxed and focused state, a state in which it can be most effective.

CUES

1. Write a specific description of the problem in as objective a way as possible.

2. Brainstorm as many solutions as you can. Do not critique, filter out, or censor your ideas; be spontaneous and unconventional. Consider asking someone you trust to work with you to add more options to your list. Be open minded.

3. Seek out a variety of perspectives. Use critical thinking and reasoning, and seek out clear, relevant, and accurate solutions. Critically evaluate the pros and cons of the top three or four solutions you came up with.

@ WEB LINKS

Goal Setting

- Debtors Anonymous. This resource provides help for those who suffer from serious issues concerning unmanageable debt. www.debtorsanonymous.org
- Kiplinger. This site provides help setting up budget worksheets. www.kiplinger.com/tools/budget
- Mint. This site is an online money manager. www.mint.com

4. Pick one solution you wish to work on at this time. You can always come back to the others.

5. Write a specific action step you will commit to: *I will* _____.

FINISH

Take a few deep, relaxing breaths. Picture yourself taking your action step and succeeding. How can you use this method to come up with solutions or at least actions you can take to resolve other problems?

Time Management = Self-Management

College students often feel stressed because of a lack of time to get everything done. People use the term *time management* in such situation, but this term may be a misnomer. We all have the same amount of time: we can't get more of it. A better term might be *self-management*. If you are having time issues, rather than trying to manage your time, consider managing yourself instead. The dilemma is not so much about a lack of time, but rather about wasting energy (physically, emotionally, and intellectually) on tasks that take away from what is really important. The key to time management is seeking balance and focus. Your time is valuable, and you need to spend it carefully so you will have enough time to reach all the goals you have set.

Procrastination

Procrastination—putting off immediate action on a task—is a common time management issue for students. Many even fight for their right to procrastinate because of the secondary gains they get from not doing anything! Go figure. Here are some common mistaken beliefs regarding procrastination:

- *I perform better under pressure.* Some students believe they do their best work at the last minute, but this is rarely the case. High-quality work requires planning and preparation, and enough time for reviewing.

- *I don't have enough time.* Students often excuse their own poor time management skills by saying they were not given enough time to complete an assignment.

- *If I don't do it, someone else will, so why bother?* Procrastination often results in others having to pick up the slack. However, relationships require all parties to bring their best skills to the task. Those who don't "show up" never get better at these skills, never learn new ones, and don't experience what it is like to contribute to a team.

Some good self-management suggestions come from students like you who have faced some of the same situations that you might be facing. Here are some suggestions that you might be able to put to use:

- Create a baseline time log. Choose a few typical weekdays and one weekend day and log all the activities you do. Review your time log and look for time zappers—time spent with little or no return. Downtime for relaxation is fine, but consider where you may be wasting time (e.g., taking naps, playing video games, or watching TV between classes). Are you bored or unmotivated at certain times of the day?

- Take a critical look at your study work space. Is your room full of distractions such as people coming in and out, the TV on and phones ringing, and food scattered about? If so, find a quiet, controlled study space such as the library or a study hall.

- Schedule study time for the time of day when are you at the top of your game (i.e., most alert and productive).

- Break your goals down into smaller realistic and attainable steps. Success encourages future success. Each week, review your goals and make a to-do list of the manageable steps you need to take that week.

- Use only one planner system. Coordinating a paper planner with a phone app can be difficult. Put everything you need to remember and track into one system.

- Each day, do the most important and challenging thing on your to-do list first.

- Know your window of opportunity—that is, how long you can concentrate on a difficult task such as reading. Instead of scheduling a grueling all-nighter, set aside blocks of time such as 15 minutes, 20 minutes, and one half hour to do one thing only. Then use the rest of your study time to mix in other tasks such as recopying notes, outlining a paper, and writing out flash cards.

- Take breaks! Intersperse fun tasks that engage other areas of your brain into your study time. Play Sudoku (looking for number patterns) when you are writing a paper, or take some time to work out or talk to a friend. Watch a funny sitcom. Set a timer so you get back to your work plan when your break is over.

- Review class material every day, not just before the test. Use flash cards to review the most important aspects of the material.

- Cross-train (i.e., use more than one method to study). Instead of reading over your notes, make flash cards, read your notes out loud, make audio recordings of key concepts to review, quiz yourself on key concepts and terms, and visualize key concepts.

- Shut off interruptions. Multitasking is a difficult habit to break. Doing several tasks at once or allowing interruptions pulls you away from doing one thing with full concentration and focus. Consider setting aside 30 minutes with no technological interruptions. Turn off the electronics.

- Join a study group of people who are committed to doing their best. Show up prepared and on time to scheduled meetings. Quiz each other and discuss concepts to hear a variety of ways to consider the subject material.

- Don't take notes; sit and listen rather than writing furiously. Trust that you can take in the information.

- Investigate apps for your phone that you can use to keep organized. Assignment Planner is a free app that helps you plan your entire course load across the semester. https://play.google.com/store/apps/details?id=gene.android

@ WEB LINK

Time Management

Time management help.com. This site offers specific tips on time management for college students. www.timemanagementhelp.com

MANAGING YOUR TIME JOURNAL ACTIVITY

This activity helps you organize your time and find a time management system you can use consistently.

START

Mindful sitting with journal

CUES

1. Make a list of the things you did in the past 48 hours (besides sleeping and eating). File each activity into one of four files:
   - File 1: Important and urgent
   - File 2: Important but not urgent
   - File 3: Not important but urgent
   - File 4: Not important and not urgent

2. Examine how much of your time was spent doing things you placed in files 3 and 4. For example, in file 3 there is a homework assignment that you did not think was important or interesting; you procrastinated on it, and it then became urgent and you rushed through it to get it done. Notice if you spend a lot of time in the "time zappers" zone (i.e., activities in file 4 such as watching TV and hanging out). Identify your typical procrastination traps.

FINISH

List steps you can take to reduce stress and increase productivity. Set a goal to commit to one of those steps.

PLANNING FOR TOMORROW

This activity helps you to mindfully plan so you can achieve your goals for tomorrow.

START

Mindful sitting with journal

CUES

1. What are the most important things you need to do tomorrow? List the top five.
2. Decide which of the things you have prioritized for tomorrow is the one you should do first.
3. Set an intention to do your best in accomplishing this task before you move on to something else or become distracted.
4. Remind yourself of your intention to put all of your energy, attention, and commitment toward this important goal.

FINISH

Take a deep breath and make a sincere effort to let go of this list for now. Leave the journal at your workplace or wherever you will see it first thing in the morning to bring you into focus and remind you of your commitment (e.g., in your backpack ready to look at in the morning). Walk away knowing you will be ready to do your best.

Self-Discipline

Self-discipline is twice as strong as intelligence as a predictor of academic success (Seligman, 2011). Consider the 10,000 hour rule developed by Malcolm Gladwell (2008), who wrote the book *Outliers*. He observed successful people and found that they persevered in their efforts toward their goals. He proposed the 10,000 rule based on many case studies, and that rule says that 10,000 hours of work toward a goal are needed to achieve success at a task. Steve Jobs (2009) echoed this advice in an interview about his and others' success; he said that successful people love and have a passion for what they pursue. The point is that taking consistent actions toward your goal is the key to success—you have the power to make it happen through your attitude and passion toward your goals.

> *We are what we repeatedly do. Excellence, then, is not an act, but a habit.*
>
> Aristotle

Daniel Pink wrote in *Drive: The Surprising Truth About What Motivates Us* (2011) about the science of motivation and the application to many areas including business, education, and personal life. The perception of motivation as a desire to reap rewards and avoid punishment is outdated. Pink focused on the important concept of *intrinsic motivation*: being motivated by our own interest and passion rather than something outside of us. He has found the following elements to be essential to achieving true intrinsic motivation:

- *Autonomy:* Be the director of your own life.
- *Mastery:* Get better at something that matters to you.
- *Purpose:* Be part of something bigger than you.

Pink's views are supported by much of the research on optimism, happiness, flow, mindfulness, meaningful engagement, locus of control, altruism, and creativity presented in this chapter.

Creative Imagination

The power of our brain to imagine and be creative is astounding. However, we can also imagine the absolute worst-case scenario and create all kinds of drama in our

@ WEB LINKS

Self-Discipline

- Daniel H. Pink. This site provides a survey on drive, or intrinsic motivation. www.danpink.com/drivesurvey
- Daniel H. Pink. Pink's website also offers an e-mail newsletter that reports on updates on the science and practice of motivation. www.danpink.com/email-newsletter

Reminiscing about fun and happy times from your past can be an instant boost to your mood.

minds, which can be detrimental to our health. Creative imagination works on the premise that the brain doesn't differentiate between reality and imagination. Let's test this premise. Take a moment and imagine that you have sliced open a fresh lemon. You hold a wedge of the cool lemon in your hand and bring it your mouth. Take a big bite into the lemon wedge feeling the lemon juices squirt out. Is there a real lemon in your hand? However, did your body respond as if there were? Did you salivate and scrunch up your face into a pucker?

Creative imagination taps into the subconscious brain, where feelings and memories are stored. This vast resource offers endless possibilities for healing and achieving positive outcomes. This power of the subconscious is the reason that 10 minutes of meditation or creative imagination can be as restorative to the body as several hours of restful sleep.

The tool of visualization uses only one sense—sight. In creative imagination, however, we use as many senses as possible to engage the prefrontal cortex, or higher brain. This sends messages to the lower brain areas that control emotions and reactive responding that all is well!

The following list provides some keys to using your creative imagination.

- Come into deep relaxation. This will allow you to access both hemispheres of the brain.

- Act "as if"—use the present tense in describing your imagery. Say to yourself: *I am _____.*

- Use as many senses as possible. Make the imagery rich and full of interesting details of smell, sound, touch, taste, image, emotions, and texture.

- Elicit positive feelings in your imagination. The brain remembers things that are associated with strong positive emotions.

- Be unlimited in your imagination. If you want to fly, then fly! There are no barriers in this realm.

- Make your imagined reality your own; don't censor or limit yourself by imagining what others might think.

Example of a Creative Imagination Script to Prepare for a Presentation

Step 1

Take a moment to become centered and grounded. Find a seated position that is comfortable. Sit up as tall and strong as you comfortably can; let your spine grow long and sit firmly on both sit bones.

Step 2

Close your eyes if you feel comfortable doing so, or just keep a relaxed eye gaze. Take five deep and relaxing breaths. You have worked hard getting ready for this presentation and are looking forward to doing your best.

Step 3

1. Set your intention. What is your goal? Select a few choice words that are significant and convey your intention (e.g., *confidence, flow, enjoyment*). Take a few more moments to zero in on your intention. Make it simple and clear and use positive language in stating it (e.g., *During my presentation, I will clearly voice all my talking points*).

2. Use your imagination and creativity to picture your presentation on a big screen. Imagine the room, people in the audience, what you are wearing. Add sounds, including the sound of your strong voice. What does it feel it like to be there? What is the temperature of the room? Imagine your body feeling at ease and confident. Take a few more moments to put in more details such as the physical sensation of taking a sip of water. The more detailed and realistic your imagined scenario is, the better.

3. Now picture yourself in a situation that is challenging and disturbs your presentation, such as forgetting where you are or stumbling on words when asked a question. Consider whatever might upset your ability to stay grounded, centered, in your breath, and totally devoted to your goal.

4. Instead, in your mind's eye, see yourself, hear yourself, feel yourself executing the perfect presentation. Run through this perfect situation as if you can hit *Replay* over and over again. If any doubt or failure or *yeah but* or *I never* tries to break through, turn this down as you would turn down the volume on your iPod. Run this perfect tape with all the imagination and creativity you can. Really enjoy the feeling of confidence, calm, and equanimity.

5. Repeat your intention several times to yourself. Take five more relaxed breaths. Revisit your tall and strong posture. Slowly open your eyes and come back to the room you are in. You are relaxed and refreshed and pumped to do your very best in your presentation.

Step 4

Reflect on how practicing your presentation using creative imagination could help your presentation performance.

@ WEB LINK

Creative Imagination

Weil. Andrew Weil is a medical doctor who pioneered work in complementary medicine and uses creative imagination extensively with his patients. www.drweil.com

MAPPING

There are online programs that allow you to view aerial images of geographical areas, businesses, even your house and street. For example, Flash Earth allows you to click anywhere in the world and see the geographical area from satellite and aerial images (www.flashearth.com). In this creative imagination activity, you imagine you have a camera that is focused on you and then slowly pull the focus back into space.

START

Relaxation pose or mindful sitting

CUES

1. Imagine a camera focused on you as you lie in relaxation pose or sit upright in a relaxed and comfortable position. Be very calm and still as you use creative imagination to view a very calm and relaxed scene.
2. Slowly allow the camera lens to pull back, seeing the house or building you are in, or if outside, the area around where you are seated or lying.
3. As the lens pulls back even farther, see the street, the block, and the town or city you are in . . . the state . . . the region . . . the hemisphere . . . and now, finally, the earth.
4. Allow yourself to enjoy viewing the earth from this vantage point of spaciousness and ease. Continue to enjoy this calm and relaxed view.

FINISH

Take a few moments to take in the sense of relaxation and calm you have created.

STAIRWAY

The jury is still out on what the famous song "Stairway to Heaven" of the 1970s means, but it is still iconic today—over 40 years later. In this creative imagination activity, you will imagine taking steps up a stairway to a place of comfort and relaxation.

START

Relaxation pose or mindful sitting

CUES

1. Imagine a stairway in front of you. Take a deep breath as you prepare to take your first step.
2. As you take your first step up the stairway, feel yourself becoming more relaxed.
3. With your next step, imagine that you are weightless and that each subsequent step is effortless.
4. As you reach the top of the stairs, there is a comfortable platform on which to relax. Take a seat in a comfortable chair and gaze out at the view from a tower, the top of a lighthouse, or the summit of a mountain. Continue to gaze out at the relaxing view.

FINISH

Take a few moments to soak in the creative imagination you have produced.

Note: If another image is more conducive to helping you relax, then substitute it in the activity—perhaps taking an escalator or flying on the back of a bird as you ascend to each level or floor and become more and more relaxed.

WHEN I WAS YOUNG

In this creative imagination activity, you capture a time in your life as a young child. Pick a time when you were carefree, happy, and absorbed in play or an activity.

START

Mindful sitting or relaxation pose

CUES

1. Set the scene for remembering a happy and carefree time in your life.
2. Watch yourself at play or involved in an activity. Use as many of your senses as possible to recreate this scene.
3. Smile and tell this child that he or she is safe and loved unconditionally.
4. Continue to spend time in this happy and carefree moment with your inner child.

FINISH

Reflect on how imagining being a kid again and enjoying life and being happy makes you feel.

COMPLAIN ABOUT IT AND MOVE ON

Although it may sound strange, we sometimes find comfort, or at least some sort of satisfaction, in ruminating about a situation; we enjoy staying stuck in it. This attitude of complaining may feel good and help us process the situation in some way, but at some point we need to take action to make the situation better or just let it go and move on.

START

Mindful sitting

CUES

1. Bring to mind a situation that is frustrating you. Give yourself permission to think of all the things about it that annoy you and let yourself complain. Continue until your complaints run out or for about one minute, and then stop.
2. Now imagine that you have pushed the stop or pause button on this situation. Take a few deep breaths. Try to come up with at least one positive thing about the situation.
3. Set an action step you can commit to, to improve this situation. It may just be an intention to let it go.

FINISH

Reflect on your ability to complain about a situation but also to see the silver lining and possible ways to deal with it.

COUNTING FIVE

In this activity you use your fingers to hold on to relaxing, heartfelt images.

START

Mindful sitting; you can either look at your hand or picture it in your mind.

CUES

1. Focus on your thumb and imagine all the people in your life who love and support you.
2. Focus on your index finger and imagine a time when you felt special and unique.
3. Focus on your middle finger and imagine a time when you did something for someone else without being asked or expecting a reward.
4. Focus on your ring finger and imagine a variety of ways you are creative, and what fuels your creativity.
5. Focus on your little finger and imagine how appreciative you are of your authentic, true nature.

FINISH

Take a few minutes to just focus on your whole hand as warm and relaxed and at ease.

BLUEPRINT

During this activity you plan all the steps toward achieving a goal. Think back to a time-lapse video you have seen of a concert being set up or a building being built to illustrate the many steps required to make a goal happen. This is what you will do with an important goal you wish to accomplish.

START

Mindful sitting

CUES

1. Imagine a goal you wish to accomplish. Be very clear about how accomplishing this goal will look, sound, taste, feel, and smell.
2. Focus on the positive emotions of pride, motivation, and a sense of accomplishment. Just like time-lapse photography, imagine the process of taking each of the small steps necessary to accomplish your goal.
3. Make sure to include images of all the successive steps required and make them as detailed as possible.

FINISH

As you slowly open your eyes, take three deep breaths. Take out a piece of paper or your journal and write down your goal and the action steps needed for accomplishing it. When goals are written down in conjunction with using creative imagination, powerful intentions to fulfill those goals are set in motion.

GETTING RID OF STRESS USING STRESS BALLS

Using stress balls is a tactile technique for relieving stress. Stress balls can be purchased or can be made from heavy-gauge balloons or surgical gloves filled with rice, small beans, or lentils. Use a funnel to fill up the balloons or gloves and tie them off.

START

Mindful sitting with a stress ball

CUES

1. Take a moment to focus on all the stress or worries you are concerned about right now.
2. As you slowly squeeze your stress ball with your nondominant hand, imagine your stress or concerns draining out of your hand and into the stress ball. Empty all of your stress into your stress ball.
3. As you slowly relax your hand, imagine all of your stress or concerns draining out of the stress ball and just evaporating.
4. Repeat several times until all your stress has dissolved.

FINISH

Take a few deep, relaxing breaths. Consider using a stress ball before an exam or while waiting for an appointment.

USING METAPHOR

This creative imagination activity uses the power of metaphor to help you let go of negative qualities and cultivate positive qualities such as strength, relaxation, and peace. These images will add richness and meaning to the practice of creative imagination.

START

Mindful sitting

CUES

1. Imagine the colors red and black representing tension and stress. Allow them to soften and disappear into the relaxing colors of blue and white.
2. Imagine a taut, coarse piece of rope representing tension. Allow this rope to gently unravel into a ball of silky-smooth, beautiful yarn.
3. Imagine the sound of a jarring alarm clock representing stress, and allow this sound to slowly dissipate into the sound of a soft, gurgling brook.
4. Imagine the bright, obnoxious glare of high beams as tension, and allow this image to fade into a gentle light coming over the horizon at daybreak.
5. Imagine a clear, placid lake. See beautiful stones at the bottom of the lake. Imagine the lake becoming frozen or agitated with choppy waves, making it difficult to see the beautiful stones. Now imagine the water becoming still and quiet so you can see the stones again.
6. Imagine a spool of twine representing all your ties to your worries or to-do list. Slowly watch the twine unwind into a soft pillow where you can rest without a care in the world.

EXTENSION

Bring to mind an object or aspect of nature—something that represents a quality you wish to bring to your attention (e.g., colors, clouds, sun rays, bubbles, a mountain, a trickling brook). Continue to focus on this image.

FINISH

Think about how other examples such as photographs, body art, sound recording, or jewelry can act as images and sounds that could represent qualities you want to cultivate.

WISE SAGE

This activity uses imagination to tap into your intuition, or inner wisdom.

START

Mindful sitting or relaxation pose

CUES

1. Lie or sit quietly and take a few relaxed breaths. Focus on a problem you are working on.
2. Imagine a knock on the door. You open the door and a trusted wise person is standing there. This person is eager to help you with your problem. Invite him or her in and sit together for a few deep breaths. Allow this wise person to help you with your problem; imagine handing it over to him or her.
3. Listen to the advice the person offers. Watch the person hand the problem back to you and tell you that you are now ready to work on it. Walk the wise person to the door and thank him or her for visiting and helping you out.
4. As you sit back down, realize that you had the wisdom and inner knowing all along. You have the all answers you need. Remember to take the time to quiet down enough to listen to the answers that are best for you.

FINISH

Take the time now to reflect on your inner wisdom and the need to trust your intuition.

BUBBLE THINKING

This activity brings your awareness to your random thoughts. Instead of staying stuck with a thought and ruminating on it or getting carried away with it, you can put it into a soap bubble and watch it float away.

START

Mindful sitting

CUES

1. Sit quietly.
2. As you notice any thoughts, imagine putting each one into a soap bubble. The bubbles bobble for a few moments and then float up and drift away.
3. Continue to place any thoughts into bubbles and send them away in the breeze.

FINISH

Enjoy the relaxed and calm mind-set you have created by letting your thoughts just drift away.

BURNING A CANDLE

In this activity you imagine lighting a candle and paying attention to all the senses involved when you watch the wax melt.

START

Mindful sitting

CUES

1. Imagine sitting at a table with a candle and a book of matches.
2. Light a match (smell the sulfur) and hear the match strike. Watch as you light the wick and the wick flickers and ignites into a candle flame.
3. Smell the candle wax.
4. See the small pool of wax slowly build up until it starts to spill over the candle edge like the tension in your body or mind. Just watch each drop of wax escape, drip, and slide down.
5. Imagine all the tension and worries in your mind and body draining away and escaping, dripping and sliding away just like the candle wax.
6. Blow out the candle and rest quietly in the dark.

FINISH

Sit for a few deep breaths and enjoy the feeling of relaxation and calm you have created.

GETTING ON TARGET FOR ATHLETES

In this activity you create a mind-set for optimal performance and then recall it in the actual situation. It can be modified for any kind of performance.

START

Mindful sitting or relaxation pose

CUES

1. Recall a peak experience in which you achieved optimal performance in your sport and assign it a number on a scale of 1 to 10—1 representing sound, restful sleep and 10 representing total chaos and feeling out of control. Remember how it felt to be in that moment of perfect execution of the skills needed and give it a number.
2. Continue to keep in your mind this number (called your target number) and bring as much detail as possible to remembering your peak performance.

FINISH

Take a few more deep breaths and keep in mind your target number. The next time you are preparing for sport, recall this image and your target number. Ask yourself continually throughout your performance if you are on target. If you are over this target number, take the time you need to calm down, focus, and relax so you can come back to this target and optimal performance.

BEAM OF LIGHT

In this activity you use a beam of light similar to that of a flashlight as a focal point while slowly bringing attention and relaxation to various areas of your body.

START

Mindful sitting or relaxation pose

CUES

1. Imagine a beam of light as your focus tool.
2. Bring this beam of light to your head. Focus all your attention on the beam as it illuminates your head area. Notice all of your sensations, feelings, and thoughts. Let them all go.
3. Move the beam of light from your head slowly and methodically to other areas of your body in increments of 12 inches (30 cm), taking a few deep breaths at each area. Notice and accept any sensations, feelings, or thoughts that come up as the light beam shines on each area. If you notice nothing, accept that as well. Then let it all go.

FINISH

Take a few moments and rest quietly before coming back to the room and your day. Notice how you feel after completing this meditation activity.

WRITING YOUR OWN SCRIPT

In this activity you create a guided imagination script to use as a stress management tool. You then read your script to a partner and ask for feedback to make the script better. You might want to record your script (e.g., as an MP3 file) to listen to later when you are feeling stressed.

START

Mindful sitting with journal or computer

CUES

1. Find a theme that you want to use in your guided imagination script. Review the themes provided in this chapter such as nature or a relaxation spot, but also consider an imaginary place (e.g., a magic carpet ride or a lunar walk).
2. Brainstorm ideas to use in your script. List words for each of the following areas:
   - Sights and colors (e.g., multicolored leaves on a fall day, brilliant sunset on the horizon)
   - Textures, temperature (e.g., warm sand under your feet; the cool, crisp feel of winter air on top of a ski slope)
   - Sounds (e.g., music, birds chirping)
   - Tastes (e.g., salt air, sweat)

- Smells (e.g., a pine forest, popcorn at a fair)
- Other people or animals (e.g., people walking on a beach, chipmunks scattering on a hiking path)
- Movement (e.g., leaves rustling in the trees, wind blowing through your hair)
- Feelings (e.g., invigorated, calm, peaceful)

3. From your list of words, start writing your script; include pauses.
4. Read your script out loud to yourself to make sure the language is authentic and meaningful to you. The script should be rich with language to evoke all the senses but also include enough pauses to give yourself or your partner time to process and experience the guided imagination.

FINISH

Consider reading your script to a classmate or friend and get feedback about its usefulness as a stress management tool. Record your script so you can listen to it when you need a stress management break.

Summary

The power of thoughts to influence our health and wellness is an exciting and important area of research today. This chapter addressed the leading areas in this growing field of mind–body connection: mindfulness, meditation, self-management, reframing, disputation, affirmations, goal setting, problem solving, and creative imagination. Chapter 5 addresses stress management in the dimension of social wellness.

Believe in your dreams.

Believe in today.

Believe that you are loved.

Believe you can make a difference.

Believe we can make a better world.

Believe when others might not.

Believe there's a light at the end of the tunnel.

Believe that you might be that light for someone else.

Believe that the best is yet to be.

Believe in each other.

Believe in yourself.

I believe in you.

Kobi Yamada, 2009

stress

chapter 5

Social Wellness

The creation of a more peaceful and happier society has to begin from the level of the individual and from there it can expand to one's family, to one's neighborhood, to one's community, and so on.

Dalai Lama

Social support refers to the quality of our relationships. According to most researchers, it is defined as "the degree to which a person's basic social needs are met through interaction with other people" (Karren et al., 2010). Social support includes feeling cared for, feeling loved, and having mutual obligations with others in the group. The best role models of social support in the animal kingdom are penguins. During the harsh winter months, they support and protect each other by taking turns being on the outside of the group huddle.

Social support can be obtained from a variety of sources:

- *Providers.* These are people who offer material support such as money or the loan of a car.

- *Disclosers.* With these people we feel comfortable sharing important information in confidence.

- *Guides.* Guides are those we can ask for advice without feeling obligated to take that advice.

- *Energizers.* People in our lives who have a positive outlook, keep us moving toward optimism, and encourage positive healthy behaviors energize and motivate us.

- *Rocks.* Some people in our lives are there when we need help and loyal no matter what. We share a mutual sense of responsibility with people we consider our rocks.

Negative issues related to social wellness include poverty, overcrowding, homelessness, dangerous living conditions, financial uncertainty, discrimination, and loneliness. An issue that many college students experience in the dimension of social wellness is loneliness. The Alameda County Study (see the sidebar) and numerous other studies support the idea that loneliness is detrimental to our health. Friends help buffer the effects of stress. It is important when coming onto campus as a first-year student, a transfer student, or a nontraditional student to feel connected.

@ WEB LINK

Social Support

The Cancer Support Community is a national organization providing advocacy for cancer patients and stress reduction. This is an example of social support. www.cancersupportcommunity.org

Commuter, working, and married students can be especially vulnerable to feeling isolated. Suggestions to offset loneliness provided by students include joining a club (like campus and community organizations), volunteering in community service, participating in extra projects in your major such as research or a professional fraternity, and getting involved in campus extracurricular activities such as recreation leagues. The following list contains some more suggestions for making new friends.

- Accept invitations to events, even if you feel awkward and reluctant at first.
- Don't wait to be invited somewhere. Take the initiative and ask someone.
- Strike up a conversation with the person next to you in class or at a local gathering. You could be introducing yourself to a new friend.
- Talk about things that interest other people. Develop your rapport skills: be an attentive listener, use nonverbal listening skills such as eye contact, and use positive language (Goleman, 2011).
- If you live in a residence hall, take advantage of group activities to meet people or to be physically active, such as participating on an intramural activity team.
- Find people who also have an interest in developing healthy lifestyle behaviors and get involved in activities with them. Join the hiking club or other outdoor interest groups.

Another area of stress common to many college students is parental stress. Although parents can be a significant source of social support, they can also be a source of stress. Some parents have difficulty letting go of their children and continue to hover and try to control their lives when they enter college. Setting healthy boundaries is an important skill within all relationships. Following are suggestions by students for setting boundaries with parents:

- Take the time to talk with your parents when it is best for you—not during a class or while you are studying.
- Ask for help when you need it, but take responsibility for your own decisions.
- Thank your parents for their help and advice.
- Limit your dependence. Do not whine about an issue before taking some time to try to figure it out for yourself.
- Make sure family members know that school is a priority and that you cannot do errands or help out when you have school obligations.

◉ FOCUS on Research

Alameda County (California) Study

This classic study investigated two groups of people: those with high levels of social support and those with low levels. Those with lower levels of social support had three times the rate of death. These results endured when the researchers conducted a follow-up 17 years later. Even when they took into consideration other factors such as smoking, inactivity, and obesity, a low level of social support was still a risk factor for death.

Berkman & Sym, 1979.

Sources of Social Support Scale (SSSS)

The Sources of Social Support Scale (SSSS) was used with women diagnosed with breast cancer. It has a section for each source of support being assessed. Each section uses essentially the same questions regarding the kind of help and support the respondents receive. Respondents choose from the following choices for each question:

1 = Not at all

2 = A little

3 = A moderate amount

4 = A pretty large amount

5 = A lot

The first section concerns the respondent's husband or partner (if the respondent is in an intimate relationship). Here are the questions:

1. How much does your husband or partner give you advice or information about your breast cancer (whether you want it or not)?
2. How much does your husband or partner give you assistance with things related to your breast cancer (for example, helping you with daily chores, driving you places, dealing with bills and paperwork)?
3. How much does your husband or partner give you reassurance, encouragement, and emotional support (affection) concerning your breast cancer?
4. How much does your husband or partner listen to and try to understand your worries about your breast cancer?
5. How much can you relax and be yourself around your husband or partner?
6. How much can you open up to your husband or partner if you need to talk about your worries about your cancer?
7. How often does your husband or partner argue with you relating to your cancer?
8. How often does your husband or partner criticize you relating to your cancer?
9. How often does your husband or partner let you down when you are counting on him or her?
10. How often does your husband or partner withdraw from discussions about your illness or try to change the topic away from your illness?

Subsequent sections address other family members, friends, and health care providers.

Reprinted, by permission, from C.S. Carver, 2006, *SSSS (Sources of Social Support Scale)* (Miami, FL: University of Miami, Department of Psychology). Available: www.psy.miami.edu/faculty/ccarver/sclSSSS.html

What kind of a friend are you? Are you supportive? Do you allow friends to support you? Can you listen? Can you laugh?

HOW CAN I BE A BETTER FRIEND?

Using the list provided, reflect on the assets of your best friend and consider how you might be a better friend.

START

Mindful sitting with journal

CUES

Reflect on each of the following adjectives to assess what your best friends and you bring to your relationships.

- Present—Have an ability to be present, comfortable, and relaxed.
- Trustworthy and respectful—Are worthy of confidence as a result of validating friends' thoughts and feelings.
- Nonjudgmental—Encourage a feeling of being accepted no matter what.
- Reliable—Are dependable when needed.
- Reciprocal—Share equally in the relationship; expectations are realistic.
- Lighthearted—Can laugh with friends to lighten things up; don't use humor maliciously.

FINISH

What step would you be willing to take to be a better friend?

JOURNALING ABOUT SOCIAL SUPPORT SOURCES

Take a look at the sources of social support listed at the start of the chapter as you complete this journal activity.

137

START

Mindful sitting with journal

CUES

1. Whom do you look to for support in each of these categories?
2. How do you provide social support in each of these categories?
3. Is there an action step you could take to strengthen your ability to seek as well as provide social support?

FINISH

Set an intention to take an action step toward improving your ability to provide social support.

JOURNALING ABOUT INCREASING YOUR SOCIAL SUPPORT SYSTEM

In this activity you explore ways to improve your social support system.

START

Mindful sitting with journal

CUES

Consider the following questions and write your thoughts in your journal.

- How would you define a true friend?
- Are there areas of interest you could explore to meet new friends?
- Are there role models you can look to that epitomize friendship?
- Can you get involved in a community service project where you might meet other people involved in worthwhile projects?
- Can you work on your own skill at being honest and not hurtful?
- Can you set healthy boundaries such as setting aside alone time, studying uninterrupted, and not sending texts during sleep hours?
- How can you foster better emotional and social intelligence "interdependence" where you accomplish more when you give and receive help?

FINISH

Set an intention to take an action step toward improving your social support system.

Intimate Partner Relationships

The source of stress most often cited by students is intimate partner relationships (i.e., boyfriends or girlfriends). Much of the struggle in relationships revolves around power and control. We often feel pressure to be in intimate relationships, but research shows that being in unhappy relationships can wreak havoc on our wellness.

To cultivate a healthy relationship, ask yourself and your partner the following questions:

- What is important in the relationship?

- Does the relationship have more pluses than minuses? A 5:1 ratio makes for a happy relationship. This means that for every negative issue, there are five words or acts of love such as signs of affection, humor, surprise, touch, thoughtful planning, and communication.

- Do you share the responsibility for keeping the relationship healthy and happy?

- When you interact, are you both aware of attitude, negativity, whining, blaming, having to be right, tone, and language? Do you listen and use reflective responses to indicate that you've listened for not only content but also feelings?

- Do you ask hard questions (e.g., whether your partner has been tested for STIs or is committed to a sexually monogamous relationship) and listen to answers you may not want to hear?

- If you have had issues or arguments in the past, did you or partner act respectfully? If there was a breakup, were you both honest? Did you speak directly, or was there a text to communicate that the relationship was over?

Repeat what you say three times: once for each ear and again for the heart.

Author unknown

Interpersonal Communication

A great deal of stress is caused by miscommunication. Understanding our own feelings and then describing or expressing them can be difficult especially when feeling stressed, intimidated, or put on the spot. We fail to communicate when we don't speak directly to people, talk in circles to avoid saying what needs to be said, relay unclear messages, avoid conversation, or send messages electronically. Taking the time to be clear about feelings and communicating them to others is a big step in managing stress. Communication is an important lifelong skill. It includes active listening and mindful responding, as well as committing to being honest, trustworthy, and empathetic. Also keep in mind that a great deal of communication is nonverbal: our body language and facial expressions. Make sure your body language is respectful and that any physical touching of the other person conveys caring, respect, and compassion. Eye contact conveys a great deal of information—not looking at the person when you are apologizing sends much more of your message than words ever could.

An important skill in interpersonal communication is *active listening*, which involves giving your full attention to your partner. Following are guidelines for practicing active listening:

- Maintain respectful facial expressions and use eye contact. Listen not just with your ears but also with your eyes and whole body.

- Face the speaker while leaning forward with a respectful space between you.

- Make a commitment to being attentive. Make the situation as free of distractions and interruptions as possible. Turn off the phone.

- Listen for not only content but also the feelings behind the words.
- Don't interrupt. Again, don't interrupt.
- Don't fidget (e.g., tapping your fingers, jiggling your leg).
- Relax so your partner can relax as well. Nod with interest.
- Be aware of body language (e.g., crossing your arms in a defensive stance). Notice your and your partner's gestures or any physical contact between you.
- Suspend judgment until you've heard the other person out. Let go of the need to make a retort or snappy comeback.

Interpersonal communication also includes mindful and thoughtful responding. Here are some guidelines:

- Allow for pauses. Honor silence and don't feel the need to fill it up with chitchat.
- Paraphrase to make sure you understood correctly. Restate and confirm what the person is saying so you are clear, and bring up any misunderstandings to be clarified.
- Respond with authenticity, not trite words. Keep your responses simple and direct.
- Don't assume or jump to conclusions.
- Ask questions to better understand the other person's feelings; in other words, be empathetic. Use boosters (positive statements that encourage the person to continue talking and confirm that you want to hear what he or she has to say).
- Use a respectful tone and words.
- Use a relaxed pace of speech.
- Notice when you react with blame, attachment, complaint, or a negative attitude rather than making the relationship more important than being right.
- When you want to say no, mean it! Say it assertively, keep it as brief as possible, and repeat it often.

While working on improving your communication style, consider the following styles of communication:

- *Passive communication*—Being unable or unwilling to communicate feelings and thoughts.
- *Aggressive communication*—Communicating without regard for the rights of other; this style includes bullying, criticism, and disrespect.
- *Assertive communication*—Saying what you mean and meaning what you say and standing up for your rights while not impinging on the rights of others. In assertive communication, the focus is on the issues and not on attacking others.

Obviously, assertive communication involves allowing the other person to speak. The following tips can help you improve your assertive communication skills:

- Consider what is more important—the relationship or friendship, or being right?
- Keep to the topic and avoid too much information.
- Avoid the use of slang or prejudicial words.

Assertive Communication Rights

In assertive communication, both parties have the following rights:

- To say no and mean it
- To not have an answer right away
- To change your mind
- To learn from your mistakes
- To admit when you are wrong
- To ask for help
- To your opinions (but not to force them on someone else)
- To be open to change and be flexible
- To be clear, direct, and honest

- Talk in person. Interpersonal communication should happen live and not over the phone or electronically.
- Avoid focusing on the negative; instead, look for solutions. Stick to the issue rather than attacking the person.
- Listen to understand instead of pretending to listen while focusing on what you are going to say next.
- Invite the other person to clarify or go into more detail.
- Reflect what you believe to be the speaker's ideas and feeling.
- Use assertive statements such as *I* statements:
  - Speak objectively.
  - Explain how you feel in response to the other person's actions or words rather than saying that he or she made you feel this way. Use the phrase *I feel* rather than *You make me feel*.
  - State specifically what you want in the form of a request, and say how that outcome would make you feel.
  - Invite the other person to respond to your request.
  - Ask for agreement.
  - Example: *I feel* [what you are feeling], *when you* [what happened] *because* [consequences]. *I want* [request what you want the other person to do]. *Are you willing to do this?*

PRACTICING ACTIVE LISTENING

In class, pair up to practice active listening using assigned topics or the topics listed in the Cues section. Set a time frame such as one minute for each person to talk and the other to listen actively.

START

Partners are in mindful sitting facing each other.

Good communication includes both active listening *and* a willingness to be assertive in expressing yourself. Truly listen to your friends and engage in the moment, but allow yourself to speak up and take part in the conversation as well.

CUES

Active listening topics:

- The funniest situation you ever experienced
- The person you admire the most and why
- The proudest moment in your life
- Your dream career
- Your favorite memory

FINISH

After you both have had several turns practicing active listening, reflect on what your partner did to demonstrate active listening.

JOURNALING ABOUT ASSERTIVENESS IN MY LIFE

Using the chart on the Journaling About Assertiveness in My Life worksheet in the appendix, reflect on how to use assertiveness in your communication.

Journaling About Assertiveness in My Life

	Giving	Receiving
Criticism		
Acknowledging needs and rights		
Expressing negative feelings		
Expressing positive feelings		
Acknowledging compliments		
Accepting differing opinions		
Making requests		
Being fully present and not distracted		
Saying no		
Listening without interrupting		

From N. Tummers, 2013, *Stress Management: A Wellness Approach* (Champaign, IL: Human Kinetics).

The Journaling About Assertiveness in My Life worksheet can be found in the appendix.

START

Mindful sitting with journal and reproducible chart

CUES

Reflect on your ability to both give and receive in each of the areas of assertiveness.

FINISH

What action step would you be willing to take to increase your ability to communicate assertively?

Conflict Resolution

A conflict is a struggle between people who have incompatible points of view, interests, opinions, or needs. Handling conflict in health-enhancing ways is an important aspect of healthy relationships. Conflict handled constructively can actually strengthen a relationship.

Following is a step-by-step plan to help you work through conflict with another person:

1. Agree to disagree; clarify what the conflict is about.
2. What does each person want in this situation? Take turns listening carefully without interruptions.
3. Clarify your understanding of what the other person wants. Make sure to ask questions if something is not clear or you don't fully understand.
4. Consider possible solutions that might resolve the conflict.
5. Decide together which is the best solution, and agree to both do your best to resolve the conflict.
6. Decide what you both can do if this conflict happens again, or what you can do to keep it from happening again.
7. What actions are you each willing to take to heal this relationship?

WORKING THROUGH CONFLICT

In this activity, each partner will reflect individually on resolving a conflict before working together to reach a resolution.

START

Use the step-by-step plan for conflict resolution.

CUES

First, each person will reflect individually on the conflict:

- What do you want in this situation?
- Consider possible solutions that might resolve the conflict.
- What is your responsibility in this situation?

Next, partners discuss the conflict together:

- Each person states how they would like to see the conflict resolved. Clarify your understanding of what the other person wants. Make sure to ask questions if something is not clear or you don't fully understand.

- Decide together which is the best solution and agree to both do your best to resolve the conflict.
- Decide what you both can do if this conflict happens again or what you can do to keep it from happening again.
- What actions are you each willing to take to heal this relationship?

FINISH

Reflect on the process of conflict resolution and whether you were able to come to a resolution. Although resolution is the goal, the process between you may be equally important. You may agree to disagree on this particular issue or decide that you need more time to work on it.

Differences Between Men and Women

Is there a difference between men and women regarding stress and stress management? Research reveals that the answer is yes. Because they are generally smaller than men, women may be less likely to fight or flee when confronted with a stressful situation. Men may be more suited to problem solving without a lot of dialogue (i.e., *Let's get this threat resolved quickly!*). Women's traditional role of protecting children to ensure the survival of the next generation may have led to increases in parts of the female brain that govern emotion. Remember the amygdala, the part of the brain that analyzes and processes emotional situations (see chapter 1)? It turns out that this part of the brain is larger in women than it is in men. Women tend to seek emotional connections with others, and their communication style often focuses on processing and inviting others to contribute to solving problems or dealing with situations. Taylor and colleagues (2000) found that females exhibit more of what they called "tend and befriend activities." This may be due to women's higher levels of the hormones oxytocin, prolactin, and estrogen. They noted that females respond to stress by making sure that members of the family are taken care of emotionally and socially.

However, despite their sensitivity to emotional situations, females often do not have the outlet to express their feelings. Crying in public is often considered inappropriate in our culture. Hugging or showing signs of affection may be frowned on. Men as well may be culturally discouraged to show affection or be emotional.

Recognizing the differences in how men and women behave is important in understanding how our partners, peers, family members, and friends react to stress. Neither gender is superior to the other in any situation. In the context of relationships, it's important to note that all relationships involve issues of power. In partnership we experience the pull between wanting to be in control and wanting to trust our partners, between not wanting to be dominated and wanting to feel safe and protected, and between wanting a commitment and wanting freedom and a sense of autonomy.

In a *Scientific American* article titled "Girl Brain, Boy Brain?", Lise Eliot wrote that although women and men may have anatomical and physiologic differences (e.g., brain anatomy), these differences do not dictate that all men and all women behave the same way. Individual gender traits such as interpersonal communication style develop as a result of experience and modeling and are not "hard wired" or predetermined (Eliot, 2009).

"Stress in America: Our Health at Risk" released by the American Psychological Association (2012) is a nationwide survey on attitudes and perceptions of stress among U.S. adults (18 years and older). In the section on gender differences in stress and stress management, the survey revealed that females were more likely than males to report physical symptoms associated with stress. Females were also more likely to make connections with others in their lives, which was an important factor in their stress management.

⊚ FOCUS on Research

Gender Differences and Stress

A study released in 2004 examined gender differences in stress and coping in 1,566 women and 1,250 men (ages 18 to 65) from various socioeconomic backgrounds (Matud, 2004). After factoring in the influences of socioeconomic factors such as income, Matud found that women experienced higher levels of chronic stress and daily hassles than men did. Both genders experienced similar numbers of life events, but women rated their life events as more negative and less controllable than the men did. Women listed family and health-related stressful events more frequently than men did, whereas men listed relationship, finance, and work-related stressful events more frequently. Women used more emotional and avoidance coping styles and used less rational and detachment coping styles. Men were more reserved and hesitant to express or show emotions for coping. Women reported more symptoms and psychological distress than men did. The study suggested that women undergo more stress and use more emotion-focused coping than men do.

HOW MALES AND FEMALES MANAGE THEIR STRESS DIFFERENTLY— FOR GOOD AND NOT SO GOOD

In this activity, it is critical for members of both genders to see how they manage stress in positive and negative ways. Neither gender is superior or more gifted.

START

Mixed-gender teams of three or four

CUES

Discuss with your team how women and men differ in their experience of stressors, their reactions to stress, and how they manage stress both in health-enhancing and unhealthful ways. Do not assume that one gender is better than the other. Consider how these differences might be nurtured by society and not just a product of nature.

FINISH

Reflect on how an understanding and appreciation of gender differences might improve your level of social support.

@ WEB LINKS

Gender Differences

To find out more on the differences between males and females and stress, read the report released by the American Psychological Association. www.apa.org/news/press/releases/stress/gender-stress.pdf

Animal-Assisted Therapy

Pet Partners (formerly known as the Delta Society). This nonprofit organization offers certification to people and their dogs to be pet partner teams in animal-assisted therapy. You can find a pet partner team in your area at its website. www.petpartners.org

Pets offer unconditional love, fun, and opportunities for positive social interactions.

Animal-Assisted Activities

The human–animal bond is an important social relationship. Animal-assisted activities (AAA) are motivational, educational, recreational, or therapeutic opportunities that improve people's quality of life (Pet Partners, n.d.).

In the *Handbook on Animal-Assisted Therapy: Theoretical Foundation and Guidelines for Practice* (2010), Fine wrote that spending time with a therapy animal can provide physical contact, buffer stress, decrease loneliness, and help people to relax. Animal-assisted activities provide positive social interactions, thereby addressing the dimension of social wellness. Pets provide a source of positive social interaction between the pet, pet owner, and people receiving the service. Pets can be a source of unconditional listening.

Many colleges invite therapy animals onto their campuses during final exams. Because many students live in dorms without their families' canine companions, spending time with a dog can be a welcome study break. Pet Partner teams also visit hospitals, rehabilitation centers, schools, and libraries to offer activities in social engagement and give people time with nonjudgmental friends.

Summary

Social support is one of the most significant indicators of optimal health. Although the media and society may empathize being trim and fit as the most important contributor to health, social support wins out when it comes to positive health outcomes. The quality of social support is critical; this is not about how many friends you have on Facebook. Seeking social support as well as serving as a source of social support for others are important aspirations to maintain throughout your lifetime. Consider the methods to increase your ability to provide social support given in this chapter such as active listening and mindful responding, assertive communication and conflict resolution, and understanding gender differences. Chapter 6 explores the spiritual dimension of wellness and stress management.

chapter 6

Spiritual Wellness

A human being is a part of the whole, called by us "Universe," a part limited in time and space. He experiences himself, his thoughts and feelings as something separate from the rest—a kind of optical delusion of his consciousness. The striving to free oneself from this delusion is the one issue of true religion. Not to nourish it but to try to overcome it is the way to reach the attainable measure of peace of mind.

Albert Einstein

Spiritual wellness can be difficult to define because it has many meanings (George et al., 2009). The important thing is to find a definition that best fits with your own personal beliefs. In a seven-year study titled "A National Study of Spirituality in Higher Education: Students' Search for Meaning and Purpose," researchers examined how colleges facilitated the development of students' spiritual qualities (Astin, Astin, & Lindholm, 2004). They surveyed 14,527 students attending 136 colleges and universities throughout the United States and conducted personal student and faculty interviews, focus groups, and faculty surveys. The study revealed the following spiritual qualities (Astin et al., 2004, p. 8):

- Belief in a spiritual journey—An active quest for meaning and purpose in life.
- Ethic of caring—A sense of caring and compassion for others.
- Altruistic involvement—A lifestyle that includes service to others including helping friends with problems.
- Equanimity—The capacity to maintain peace and centeredness, especially in stressful situations.
- Compassionate self-concept—The acknowledgment that one has the qualities of compassion, kindness, generosity, and forgiveness.

To return to the discussion of Maslow's hierarchy of needs in chapter 1 (Maslow, 2011), the highest point of the hierarchy is self-actualization. This means achieving our fullest potential. Spirituality is our own personal quest for self-actualization: to deepen our self-awareness and relationship with ourselves, to deepen our sense of connection with others, and to find and act on our life purpose.

Religion is an organized system of belief and practices associated with specific doctrines such as those of Christianity and Judaism. Spirituality has a much broader outlook, and one need not practice a religion to be considered spiritual. Having a religious belief system or participating in religious rituals can be part of one's personal definition of spirituality. The goal in cultivating spiritual wellness is to find practices that are authentic and meaningful to you.

The results of the National Study of Spirituality in Higher Education (Astin et al., 2004) revealed that spirituality was positively correlated with physical well-being. Specifically, students who had higher scores of spirituality were more likely than students with low scores to not drink or smoke cigarettes, have a healthy diet, and rate their health as above average. In addition, students who struggled with religious issues were more likely to stay up all night and miss school because of illness. The researchers concluded that providing students with more opportunities to connect with their "inner selves" improved their academics, leadership skills, confidence, and satisfaction with college life. The tools of meditation and self-reflection were found to be the most powerful for enhancing students' spiritual development (Astin et al., 2004).

Spirituality can be thought of as merging all the aspects of wellness into a person's life. Karren and colleagues (2010), in their book *Mind/Body Health: The Effects of Attitude, Emotions, and Relationships*, summarized the qualities of spiritual health that are found in much of what has been presented in a strengths-based approach to stress management, as follows:

- Internal locus of control—Living by our values and truths.
- Sense of meaning—Depending on the person, *meaning* can relate to family or relationships, service to others, work, or altruism. A sense of meaning can also be attributed to a religious doctrine or religious beliefs.
- Hope—A positive outlook on the future.
- Connectedness—Feeling connected to ourselves as well as to others and to a higher power.
- Forgiveness, empathy, and compassion—The ability to respond to our own suffering (self-compassion) or the suffering of others with empathy and a desire to help relieve the suffering in some way.

The choices that we make affect not only ourselves but also the people around us. If we choose to be calm and peaceful inside, we encourage a state of calm and peace in the outside world as well. Feeling separate or disconnected from our inner self can be a great source of stress.

Spiritual rituals can serve as a personal source of stress management as well as a social support when we surround ourselves with people who believe as we do. Such rituals and practices include the following:

- Take time away from our busy lives to come to a place of worship. The concept of the Sabbath in both Christianity and Judaism is about setting aside one day a week for spiritual renewal.
- Take part in traditional practices such as singing, praying, and reading inspirational passages.
- Have faith and strength when confronting life's questions about death, grief, and loss.
- Receive care and counseling from others.
- Practice healthy behaviors such as refraining from drinking or smoking, fasting, and giving up meat during Lent (in the Christian tradition).
- Help the less fortunate through service projects, altruism, and tithing.

@ WEB LINKS

Compassion and Altruism

- Center for Compassion and Altruism Research and Education (CCARE). Housed by Stanford University, this organization's mission is to research as well as find practical applications for compassion and altruistic behavior. http://ccare.stanford.edu
- The Center for Spirituality, Theology and Health. This center at Duke University focuses on research and promoting the integration of evidence-based scholarly research in the fields of religion, spirituality, and health. www.spiritualityandhealth.duke.edu

Stress Management and Spirituality Practices

Speaking conclusively about the effects of spirituality on health is difficult because spirituality is a complex and multidimensional concept (George et al., 2009). In a scholarly review of 71 research articles on spiritual health, Hawks and colleagues (1995) found that the spiritual health practices of guided imagination, meditation, and group support activities improved social, emotional, and physical health outcomes.

Prayer can serve as a kind of meditation and can be defined as focused concentration on one's personal beliefs. Both prayer and meditation are personal practices, and how we pray depends on our beliefs. Larry Dossey is a pioneer in conducting research about prayer within the medical model. In his book *Healing Words: The Power of Prayer and the Practice of Medicine* (1995), he summarized a significant amount of research evidence supporting the power of prayer to increase healthy outcomes and quality of life. Benson echoed his work when he wrote about our innate ability to heal and become whole (Benson, 2000). According to Kohls and colleagues (2011), faith in a favorable health outcome is a result of feeling empowered, having a sense of coherence, and feeling supported and secure.

Get a natural rush of feel-good endorphins simply by helping others.

Altruism

Altruism refers to service to others and a desire to contribute to something bigger than ourselves. This is different from volunteering, which people do to meet the requirements of a course or as punishment for an infraction of a law (e.g., community service hours). Community service may be forced on us, or we may consider it something helpful to add to our résumés. Altruism, on the other hand, is doing something for others without an expectation of gains, reward, or acknowledgment. The researcher Allan Luks (1988) coined the term "helper's high" to describe how altruism makes us feel good. He surveyed over 3,000 volunteers from all over the United States and found that people who helped others reported having a positive feeling or "high," felt strong and calm, and had increased energy and feelings of self-esteem as well as decreased pain and feeling of depression. Luks suggested that altruism, similar to exercise, helps combat stress by releasing endorphins—we feel better and calmer when we do something for someone else. But even better, he found that simply recalling a past altruistic act can bring about these same good feelings. Consider a service or kindness you can do on a daily basis that might make a small difference for someone else.

Forgiveness

Forgiveness is the ability to let go of hurts, grudges, or annoyances (International Forgiveness Institute, n.d.). Luskin, Ginzburg, and Thoresen (2005) found that revenge or hurtful thinking can produce the release of cortisol in the body, which has detrimental effects on our health such as a suppressed immune system. However, when people practice forgiveness, they lower their heart rate, blood pressure, perceptions of pain, and symptoms of depression.

Forgiveness is not about forgetting or condoning; rather, it is the act of letting go of the energy and ill effects of reactive stress brought on by harboring past hurts and disappointments. This can free up energy for more proactive activities. Luskin (2003) offered the following tips for practicing forgiveness:

- Take the time to put the situation into words, and find a trusted friend to discuss it with.
- Make the decision to forgive or not to forgive based on what is best for you and what will make you feel healthier.
- Forgiveness does not have to include confronting the transgressor or condoning his or her actions. Forgiveness is whatever you do to lessen the hurt, to let go of taking it personally, and to change the dialogue in your mind that causes stress.
- Keep your focus on the present. Do not launch back to the past over and over again, but view the situation from a realistic perspective in the present.
- Use stress management tools such as focused breathing, relaxation, thought stopping, and so on, to keep from escalating into stress reactivity.

@ WEB LINKS

Stress Management and Spirituality Practices

- John Templeton Foundation. This nonprofit organization conducts research into the "big questions," including life purpose and "ultimate reality." Areas of interest include creativity, forgiveness, and love. www.templeton.org
- Science of Spirituality. This nonprofit organization focuses on increasing spirituality through the practice of meditation. www.sos.org

Altruism

Altruists International. This grassroots organization promotes altruism as a social norm throughout the world. www.altruists.org/about

Forgiveness

- Learning to Forgive. The Forgiveness Project run by Frederic Luskin conducts research on forgiveness training. http://learningtoforgive.com/about
- A Campaign for Forgiveness Research. This nonprofit organization conducts research concerning forgiveness and health outcomes. www.forgiving.org

- Look at situations without expectations. Expectations are the rules we put on others that they may know nothing about or have no intention of abiding by!

- Channel your energy into positive problem solving rather than staying stuck in ruminating about the situation. Push the Forward button rather than pushing the Repeat button over and over.

- View forgiveness as a choice that gives us power to no longer let the transgressor "get to us" and to avoid the resulting stress reactivity.

Based on Luskin 2003.

WRITING A FORGIVENESS LETTER

Write a forgiveness letter to someone you are holding a grudge against. Describe how letting go of negativity and grudges and replacing them with compassion and empathy are helpful for you. You do not need to send this letter; the process of putting into words how you feel and shifting to an attitude of compassion and empathy is important for moving forward.

FORGIVENESS MEDITATION

This activity begins with an awareness of anger and resentment before opening up to forgiveness. Often, we push such negative feelings away without taking the time to explore them in a safe space.

START

Mindful sitting

CUES

1. Take five deep, relaxing breaths and let yourself become as relaxed and calm as possible.
2. Ask yourself if there is anyone you need to have a conversation with regarding your feelings of anger, hurt, or resentment.
3. Bring this person to mind. Using honest and direct language, tell this person how you feel. Do not judge or filter your words, but try to be as honest as possible.
4. If you wish, ask the person to respond with his or her point of view.

◎ FOCUS on Research

The Forgiveness Project

Fifty-five Stanford University students participated in a pilot study involving a forgiveness training program (Luskin et al., 2005). The training components included anger management and using forgiveness as a problem-solving tool. The students met for 60 minutes per week for six weeks. Compared to students in a wait list control group, students in the treatment groups significantly improved their self-efficacy, anger management, and ability to forgive. Luskin has continued his research in what he calls The Forgiveness Project.

5. Keep in mind that forgiving doesn't mean condoning what the person has done.

6. See how you feel right now and where you are in terms of your willingness to forgive.

7. Take a few breaths and open yourself to feelings of empathy and compassion for this person. If you wish, you can say "I forgive you."

You may need to go through steps 1 through 6 a few times before you are ready to do the final step of forgiving.

FINISH

Take a few deep, relaxing breaths and acknowledge your newfound sense of compassion and the work you were willing to do to forgive. Take some time to reflect on this activity—perhaps by journaling. Consider writing an affirmation of your intention to let go and let live, such as, *I forgive whoever made me feel less than I am. I can let that go now. I forgive myself and let go in peace.*

If you are finding it difficult to forgive, practice forgiving yourself. Try this affirmation: *I know I am feeling bad at this moment. I want to show loving-kindness to myself and feel unconditional love and a sense of well-being.*

Gratitude

As a result of extensive research at UCLA Davis, Robert Emmons described the qualities of people who felt a sense of gratitude as the following:

- Well-being—Positive emotions, life satisfaction, vitality, optimism, less of a focus on stress and depression
- Spirituality—Religious practices, a sense of the interconnectedness of life, commitment and responsibility to others
- Social intelligence—Empathy, an ability to see from the perspective of others, generosity, helpfulness
- Not being as materialistic—Less attachment to material goods, less inclined to be envious of others, willing to share possessions

Adapted from Emmons 2001.

In a study of 201 undergraduates, students who maintained weekly gratitude journals were found to engage in more physical activity, report fewer physical symptoms, exercise more regularly, report fewer physical symptoms, be more optimistic about the upcoming week, and feel better about their lives in general when compared to students who did not keep gratitude journals (Emmons & McCullough, 2003).

WRITING A LETTER OF GRATITUDE

In this activity you write a gratitude letter to someone who has influenced your life for the better.

START

Mindful sitting with journal or writing paper

CUES

1. Write a letter telling this person specifically what he or she did to inspire you.
2. Thank the person for this influence and say that you will strive to influence others in a positive way.

FINISH

Consider making an appointment to meet with this person and read him or her this letter.

Based on Seligman 2011.

KEEPING A GRATITUDE JOURNAL

Students have reported that keeping a gratitude journal is one of the best ways to change their attitude from seeing the world as lacking to seeing it as full of abundance and positive opportunities.

START

Mindful sitting. Use your phone, notepad, or special journal as a gratitude journal. Set aside a specific time (or times) each day to write (e.g., before meals or in the evening).

CUES

1. List everything you are grateful for today. Using words other than *grateful* may help you to convey this. If you are having difficulty being grateful, consider adopting an attitude of being grateful generally for what you have been given (with no *buts*). See if you can appreciate your blessings, people's smiles, and ah-ha moments. Here are some phrases that might help:
   - *I am grateful for _____.*
   - *I am appreciative of _____.*
   - *I am lucky to have _____.*
   - *I am thankful for _____.*
   - *I am privileged to have _____.*
2. Reflect on the word *gratitude* and what it means to you.

FINISH

When you have finished your entry, sit quietly and repeat the mantra *Thank you* for a few minutes. Set an intention to be on the lookout for gratitude tomorrow.

Additional Spiritual Wellness Practices

So far we have reviewed many of the qualities of spirituality that research has linked to stress reduction, including meditation and prayer, guided imagination, compassion, altruism, forgiveness, and gratitude. Students have also reported finding inspiration in listening to music, laughing, looking at art, spending time with inspiring people, reading inspirational words in religious texts or the biographies of inspirational people, and spending time in nature as ways to increase their spiritual health as well as manage their stress.

LOOKING FOR THE GOOD THINGS IN LIFE

This journal activity is similar to the gratitude activities, but offers a perspective that may encourage you to be more open to looking for the good things in your life.

START

Mindful sitting with journal

CUES

1. Write three to five things that went well today.
2. Reflect on why they went well.
3. Consider what you could do to make more things go well in the future.

FINISH

Reflect on what it was like to look at your day through the lens, or perspective, of finding good things. Set a goal to be on the lookout for good things throughout your day tomorrow.

Based on Seligman 2011.

WORDS TO LIVE BY

This activity is about finding words of inspiration. These words can be quotes, poems, or song lyrics. You might want to share them with the class or journal about them.

LOVING-KINDNESS MEDITATION

We must be loving and kind to ourselves before we can offer love and kindness to others. As discussed in chapter 4 in the section on negative self-talk, offering loving and kind statements to ourselves helps us to acknowledge that we are good even when we are unhappy with our behavior.

START

Mindful sitting

CUES

1. Repeat the following statements silently, pausing after each one to feel the intention behind the words:
   - *May I be happy just the way I am.*
   - *May I be at peace with whatever happens.*
   - *May I be safe and free from harm.*
   - *May I live in the wisdom of my heart.*
2. Now repeat the same statements with the intention of extending this loving-kindness to your people: family, friends, community.

- *May you be happy just the way you are.*
- *May you be at peace with whatever happens.*
- *May you be safe and free from harm.*
- *May you live in the wisdom of your heart.*

3. Now send out the words of loving-kindness to people you have had difficulty with or who have been unkind to you.
   - *May you be happy just the way you are.*
   - *May you be at peace with whatever happens.*
   - *May you be safe and free from harm.*
   - *May you live in the wisdom of your heart.*

4. Finally, send loving-kindness to all beings—animals, nature, the world, and Mother Earth.
   - *May all beings be happy.*
   - *May all beings be at peace with whatever happens.*
   - *May all beings be safe and free from harm.*
   - *May all beings live in wisdom.*

FINISH

Reflect on why it is important to send loving-kindness to yourself first. How did it feel to send loving-kindness to your immediate circle of people and also to all beings? What

You must be loving and kind to yourself before you can truly be loving and kind to others.

was it like to send loving-kindness to someone who is difficult to deal with or who has been unkind to you? Reflect on how this practice might be useful to you as a stress management tool.

SETTING A GOAL OF SPIRITUAL WELLNESS

We often set goals such as losing weight or getting a good grade in a difficult course (see the discussion of goal setting in chapter 4). However, improving our spiritual wellness is often something we aspire to but do not put our energies into. We tell ourselves we don't have enough time for it now, that we can postpone it. This activity encourages you to write a specific spiritual wellness goal and hold yourself accountable for achieving it.

START
Reflect on the qualities of spiritual wellness you may wish to explore and strengthen.

CUES
1. Select a quality of spiritual wellness to work on in the upcoming week (e.g., increasing your feelings of gratitude). Write a specific goal related to this quality, some action you can take. Start with *I will*.
2. Select a way to be accountable to reaching your goal. This may include journaling about your progress toward this goal.

FINISH
Reflect on whether you were able to manifest this goal in your life.

Summary

Spiritual wellness can be seen as the foundation of all wellness. Our highest need is often to find fulfillment in our quest to answer the big questions such as *What is my purpose on earth?* Our daily actions help us find answers to these questions. Improving our spiritual wellness can involve taking care of our physical needs, connecting with ourselves and others, having a high regard for ourselves, and taking positive steps toward realizing our highest potential. As you have journeyed through the chapters in this text, many, if not most, of the stress management activities have probably helped you in your quest toward spiritual wellness. The next and final chapter explores how our environment affects our experience of stress and how we can set up our environment to manage stress.

May the light of your soul guide you. May the light of your soul bless the work you do with the secret love and warmth of your heart.

John O'Donahue

Environmental Wellness

Slow down and enjoy life. It's not only the scenery you miss by going too fast—you also miss the sense of where you are going and why.

Eddie Cantor

this chapter addresses the environment we live in and how it can contribute to stress and our ability to manage that stress. Following are examples of sources of environmental stress:

- Technology—Middle-of-the-night text messages, a computer drive meltdown during finals.
- Light—Glare, too much high-contrast light from electronic devices, the harmful effects of tanning beds, a lack of daylight in the winter.
- Temperature—Either hot or cold (hot temperatures can increase aggressive behaviors).
- Air quality—Smells both indoors (e.g., sidestream smoke) and outdoors (e.g., pollution).
- Noise—Both intensity and source (e.g., car horns, traffic noise, high volume on an MP3 player).
- Ergonomics—Work space setup, poor posture (e.g., hunching over a laptop computer on a couch), clutter (e.g., disorganization, too much material stuff).

Stepping back and considering all the elements in the environment that are stressors and creating a healing environment can play an important role in helping us manage stress. A healing environment is one that takes into consideration all aspects of the environment listed above to create a space for optimal wellness.

Technology

Technology can be considered a double-edged sword—it can enhance our lives and make things easier or contribute significantly to our stress. Consider your own level of stress when your laptop or phone crashes! One thing to consider about technology is how it can help us feel engaged with others, such as connecting and communicating with old friends on Facebook. However, it can also be a source of stress to read about everyone having so much fun or be exposed to people being

@ WEB LINKS

Environmental Wellness

Tox Town. This site sponsored by the U.S. National Institutes of Health provides information about municipal environmental health concerns. http://toxtown.nlm.nih.gov

Television

LimiTV. This nonprofit organization encourages people to think about the issues of excessive TV watching. www.limitv.org

⊙ FOCUS on Research

Virtual Reality and Stress Management

Grassi, Gaggioli, and Riva (2009) studied the use of multimedia phones for stress reduction. A group of 120 Italian college commuters was randomly divided into three groups. Those in one group were assigned to view and listen to a video on their cell phones during their daily train commutes; those in another, to listen to audio only; and those in the third, to listen to nothing (i.e., no intervention). Compared to the audio and no intervention groups, the group that watched a video of a mountain lake along with a narrative (audio script) for relaxation experienced significant decreases in anxiety levels and increases in relaxation levels.

nasty and disrespectful. Technology can also help us manage our stress such as using a heart rate monitor during a stress management activity, listening to a favorite relaxing playlist, or keeping track of assignments using a phone app.

Television is a significant aspect of technology. Because watching an actual TV may not be the norm nowadays, the term *screen time* is more valid for referring to time tuned in to media. Watching a favorite show or comedy can be relaxing, but it needs to be in done in moderation. How much time do you spend in passive entertainment? Experts suggest that we limit screen time to less than two hours per day.

Following are negative aspects of too much screen time:

- Watching ads and infomercials touting the miracles of food products, supplements, and drugs can influence us in a negative way to use these products despite there being healthier alternatives.
- Commercials focus on our less-than-desirable attributes and can make us believe that something outside of ourselves will make us happier (e.g., the newest phone).
- Watching reality shows may provide an unrealistic view of the real world.
- Prolonged sitting can result in lethargy and a lack of energy.

According to Beresin's report "The Impact of Media Violence on Children and Adolescents: Opportunities for Clinical Interventions" (2010), watching violence on-screen has been associated with aggressive behavior, and watchers can become desensitized to violence. Another issue is that conflict resolution is not modeled on TV; children and adolescents have little exposure to seeing empathy modeled.

UNPLUGGED CHALLENGE

Often, we don't realize how much our daily lives revolve around technology until the power goes out or the battery dies on our phone or tablet. As we all know, technology can be a huge stress reliever, such as when it helps us communicate with loved ones in the middle of a crisis. But we also want to consider whether technology interferes with our quality of life. The unplugged challenge encourages you to take an honest look at the role of technology in your life and at how unplugging may change or improve it.

START

This activity has two parts—paying attention to how plugged in you are, and recognizing how being unplugged affects the quality of your life. You can record your reactions on a chart, in a log, or in a journal.

CUES

1. The first step is to honestly appraise what being plugged in means to you and the quality of your life. For example, do you text and drive? Do you play video games instead of studying? Are you constantly checking Facebook during class? Are you talking on your phone rather than being engaged in the moment at a party or event? Are you surfing websites rather than doing legitimate Web searches for your term paper? Take the time to reflect on the role technology plays in your life. Ask friends for their input. For example, you may hear from a friend how annoying it is when you are hanging out together and you are texting other people rather than giving your friend your full attention.

2. The next step is to decide on a period of time you could commit to unplugging from technology. This could be unplugging for a weekend morning, unplugging for a period of time during the day, or shutting down early in the evening. Notice how it feels to let go of technology. Ask others who might be influenced by your technology use how it feels to have a break (e.g., roommates who might be enjoying not having to listen to your phone go off incessantly while they are trying to study). Notice your stress levels while you are unplugged. At first you may become anxious as you are breaking some habits. Notice how you feel when you are not constantly checking in to see what is going on.

FINISH

After you have completed your challenge, reflect on how technology affects your level of stress. Is there a next step you might pursue, such as committing to not checking your phone during class or not texting while driving?

Light

Light can be a source of stress. Consider the strain of high-reflective light, glare, and bright ambient and artificial light, and the resulting symptoms such as eyestrain, headaches, loss of sleep, and anxiousness. When we are exposed to artificial light such as the blue light from electronic devices and LED lighting, our bodies' ability to make and use the compound melatonin can decrease causing disrupted sleep and a shift in circadian rhythms (Harvard University Newsletter, 2012). Physical, mental, and behavioral changes in humans follow a 24-hour cycle that responds predominantly to changes in light. Abnormal circadian cycles can lead to sleep disorders and other health issues such as diabetes and depression (National Institute of General Medical Sciences, n.d.). When the body is exposed to full-spectrum lighting provided by daylight and specialized lightbulbs, levels of serotonin increase. Serotonin, a neurotransmitter, helps to regulate learning, mood, and sleep. Following are ways to regulate your circadian rhythms and melatonin levels through the use of light:

- Use red lightbulbs in your nighttime reading lamps; these tend to have the least effect on melatonin suppression and shifts in circadian rhythm.

- Turn off all electronic devices several hours before going to bed.

- Increase your exposure to daylight. Research suggests that daylight exposure can improve learning (Heschong Mahone Group, 1999). According to Dartmouth University's Academic Skills Center (2012), studying during the day can result in improved retention of information.

We may feel more energized in the summer when the light is stronger and more tired or sluggish in the winter or during periods of inclement weather. According to the Yale School of Medicine's Winter Depression Research Clinic (n.d.), seasonal affective disorder (SAD) occurs during the winter months when the intensity of daylight is diminished and our exposure to natural light is shortened. Females are four times more at risk than males for SAD, with other risk factors being a family history of the disorder and living in northern climates.

Symptoms of SAD identified by Yale's Winter Depression Research Clinic (n.d.) are as follows:

- Depressed mood and fatigue
- Carbohydrate cravings, especially for sweets and starches
- Increased appetite and weight gain
- Oversleeping or having difficulty awakening in the morning
- Reduced work productivity
- Withdrawal from social contacts

Reprinted, by permission, from P. Desan, *Signs and symptoms of winter depression* (New Haven, CT: Yale School of Medicine). Available: http://psychiatry.yale.edu/research/programs/clinical_people/winter.aspx

Many of the tips for dealing with SAD are the same lifestyle practices suggested for stress management: exercise, time outdoors in natural light, and eating complex carbohydrates, especially vegetables.

Get enough light *and* beat the heat by enjoying a day with friends at the beach!

Temperature

Many of us have heard the term *the dog days of summer*. Research reveals an increase in violence during the hot months of the year (Anderson, 2001). "Keeping your cool" is an important consideration during those sweltering hot days.

Air Quality

The Air Quality Index (AQI) is a daily report on the cleanliness of the air we breathe and is based on ground-level ozone, particle pollution, carbon monoxide, and sulfur dioxide (U.S. Environmental Protection Agency, 2009). Health risks increase as the AQI increases for anyone who is active outdoors, especially children, those with "heart or lung disease (including heart failure and coronary artery disease, or asthma and chronic obstructive pulmonary disease), and older adults (who may have undiagnosed heart or lung disease" (pp. 7-8). Everyone needs to take precautions when the AQI is at high levels by limiting prolonged exposure to the outdoors and particularly heavy exertion outdoors. Additionally, it is important to consider indoor air quality in relation to issues such as sidestream smoke.

We can use our sense of smell as a stress management tool. Aromatherapy is a form of alternative medicine in which people breathe in the molecules of essential oils, which stimulate the nasal receptors to communicate with the amygdala and hippocampus, areas of the brain where emotions and memories are stored. In general, the benefits of aromatherapy are pain reduction, mood enhancement, and increases in relaxation (University of Maryland Medical Center, 2011). For example, lavender is believed to stimulate amygdala brain cells in a similar way that sedative medications do.

Another way to use scent as a stress management tool is to sprinkle or spray the blades of an inexpensive plastic fan with scented essential oils. The movement of the fan near the nostrils can have a relaxing and calming effect. High-quality candles embedded with essential oils are also available. Purchase candles made from soy or beeswax; petroleum-based candles emit harmful gases when burned. Essential oils and original scents (e.g., pine needles, dried rosemary leaves) are best for use as stress management tools. They can be purchased in health food stores and craft stores. Do not apply the oils directly to the skin because allergic reactions can occur.

Suggested Oils and Their Uses

- Calming: Lavender, vanilla, sandalwood
- Waking up: Peppermint, rosemary, lemon or orange peels
- Soothing: Ginger, pine needles

USING AROMATHERAPY FOR STRESS MANAGEMENT

In this activity you make aromatherapy sachets.

START

For the sachets you need cotton balls, essential oils or materials such as dried lavender or pine needles, 4-by-4-inch (10-by-10 cm) squares of cotton material, and yarn to tie off the sachets.

CUES

1. Apply drops of one of the essential oils to cotton balls and place several scented cotton balls (or a heaping tablespoon of dried materials) into the middle of a cloth square.

2. Gather up the corners of the cloth into the middle and tie them securely with a piece of ribbon or yarn.

3. To use your sachet, come into mindful sitting, place the sachet close to your nose, and practice a breathing, meditation, or creative imagination activity.

The cotton balls can be reapplied with the oils and stored in separate plastic bags to maintain their aroma.

FINISH

Reflect on the influence of various scents on your mood. Which one you would use in various situations? Some students have brought rosemary sachets to tests and practiced relaxing breathing using the sachets for a few minutes before the test. Many reported feeling more focused and alert during the test.

Color

A review of evidence-based research (Azeemi & Raza, 2005), revealed that color (of our environment, clothes, and even food!) can have a profound effect on our well-being. Warm colors can ameliorate symptoms of depression by encouraging activity; cool colors can evoke calmness and relaxation. According to these authors, "chromotherapy is a method of treatment that uses the visible spectrum (colors) of electromagnetic radiation to cure diseases" (p. 481).

@ WEB LINKS

Aromatherapy

- University of Maryland Medical Center. This site provides information about the medical benefits of aromatherapy. www.umm.edu/altmed/articles/aromatherapy-000347.htm#ixzz27VK7WhP5

- National Association for Holistic Aromatherapy. This nonprofit organization is dedicated to educating the public regarding the benefits of aromatherapy. www.naha.org/naha.htm

Color Tests

Max Lüscher developed the Lüscher Color Diagnostic, which has been used extensively in clinical applications since 1947. Here are two sites at which you can take color tests based on this technique:

- Color test. www.colourtest.ue-foundation.org
- Color and personality test. www.viewzone.com/luscher.html

Ergonomics

According to the U.S. Department of Labor, Office of Safety and Health Administration, (n.d.), ergonomics is the science of finding the most effective workplace conditions to encourage high productivity, decrease injury and illness, and increase satisfaction. Many of us do not optimize our work environments to do our best work or decrease distractions and disorganization. Think about how much time you waste and your frustration level when your work or study space is cluttered and disorganized and you can't find a vital piece of information.

Noise

Noise pollution refers to any sound that is unwanted or disturbing (U.S. Environmental Protection Agency [EPA], n.d.). According to the EPA, noise pollution has a direct link to "stress related illnesses, high blood pressure, speech interference, hearing loss, sleep disruption, and lost productivity." In addition, hearing loss known as noise-induced hearing loss (NIHL) is the most common health effect from noise pollution. Following are some tips for lessening the ill effects of noise pollution:

- Use ear protection around loud noise such as concerts or when using equipment such as lawn mowers and chain saws.
- Reflect on how you contribute to noise pollution by blasting your car or house stereo or setting off your car alarm.
- Turn down the volume on your personal audio devices.
- Consider drowning out annoying noise by using "white noise," which is a calming background sound such as that created by a fan.
- Practice periods of silence. Turn off the phone, radio, and TV and just enjoy the sounds of silence.

Sound

Although noise can contribute to stress, sound can be harnessed as a stress management tool. Listening to music is one of the top ways college students manage stress. The vibrating waves of sound from a relaxing playlist can bring us into an

@ WEB LINKS

Ergonomics

Virginia Tech's Cook Counseling Center. This site provides a quiz to help you evaluate your study environment to improve your productivity. www.ucc.vt.edu/stdysk/studydis.html

Noise Pollution

Noise Pollution Clearing House. This nonprofit organization has a No Noise campaign to raise awareness about noise pollution. www.nonoise.org

Healing Sounds

Jonathan Goldman's Healing Sounds. This website offers a free MP3 download of sounds to balance the body. www.healingsounds.com

experience of harmony. Given that the body is 70 percent water, it's no surprise that sound vibrations can influence our nervous system, tissues, and cells. The vibrations release endorphins, which make us feel better. Music can also make us receptive to new ideas and help us access the creative right brain.

Following are various ways to use sound in a therapeutic way:

- Listen to natural sounds (e.g., rain falling, birdsong, and animal sounds such as whales calling) either directly or on recordings.
- Listen to drumming or the sound of Himalayan singing bowls.
- Listen to instrumental acoustic tracks (i.e., music without words).
- Make music (e.g., drum, play the guitar, sing).

To use sound therapeutically, just pick something to listen to; it could be as simple as your breath or something outdoors such as rain or a bubbling water fountain. It could be silence or acoustic or classical music (without lyrics). The key is to listen without judgment or emotional attachment, to just be with the sound. As you continue to relax, use affirmations to keep you listening, such as, *The musical sounds relax me.*

USING MUSIC OR SOUNDS TO RELAX

This activity uses music and sound as a stress management tool.

START
Relaxation pose or mindful sitting

CUES
1. Your instructor will play a variety of music or sounds for the purpose of stress management. You may want to suggest tracks. Music should be without lyrics as well as slow and rhythmical.
2. Keep track of how you feel at the end of each track.
3. Raise your hand after any track that you feel was stress relieving.

FINISH
Consider sharing your playlists with other students in the class. You can provide the tracks on a sharing website such as Spotify.

Natural Surroundings

In our busy lives we often lose touch with nature. We may have entire days or longer during which we have no contact with the healing experience of nature. One solution is to bring elements from nature indoors (e.g., plants, fresh flowers, or a water fountain). Here are other ways to connect with nature:

- Study or have lunch outdoors.
- Place your table or chairs so you can get a view of the outdoors.
- Hang art that exemplifies what you love about nature.

- Listen to soundtracks of your favorite natural sound such as a babbling brook or birds chirping.
- Hang a bird feeder so you can watch birds.
- Plant a garden.

Sand Gardens

Sand gardens, in which people make patterns, are used in the East for relaxation or as a meditation focus tool. Following are the supplies needed for creating a sand garden:

Labyrinths are symbols of life's journey that can engage your creativity as you follow their paths.

- A tray with borders such as an aluminum pie plate or a small, shallow plastic tray.
- Clean sand (colored sand can be purchased at craft or dollar stores). Use about 1/2 to 1 inch (1.3 to 2.5 cm) of sand.
- A rake for making patterns in the sand. A plastic fork or a recycled fork from a tag sale would work well.
- Interesting pebbles, stones, trinkets, or other small objects to place in the sand.

Labyrinths

Labyrinths are ancient symbols used as walking paths to represent the metaphor of life's journey. The beginning and end of the labyrinth are the same point. The path consists of many turns that end at a center point, where the person then turns and rewalks the path back to the starting point. The poet T.S. Eliot captured the intention of the labyrinth with his words: "The end of all our exploring will be to arrive where we started and know the place for the first time."

Labyrinths are sometimes confused with mazes. A maze is problem to figure out, whereas a labyrinth is a tool for encouraging right brain activity such as creativity, relaxation, and imagination. More and more schools, hospitals, and health centers are including labyrinths in their environments. Typically, labyrinths are outdoors and built into natural surroundings, but some are set up indoors (see the Web Links sidebar for more information and to find labyrinths around the world).

CREATING A SPECIAL PLACE

In this creative imagination activity you imagine the soothing qualities of the outdoors.

START

Relaxation pose

CUES

1. Come into quiet, deep, relaxed breathing. Invite your eyes to close.

2. To get to your special spot, imagine getting into a car or other mode of transportation, leaving your home or school, and then traveling along a highway and then a quiet country road. Notice how the sounds of the loud cars and trucks on the highway have changed to the quiet country sounds of birds and the gravel of your tires on the country road.

3. As you arrive at your relaxing spot, you find a walking path. Step onto this path, and with each step, allow yourself to become calm and relaxed. Enjoy the quiet solitude of this outdoor space. Make a sincere effort to quiet your mind and find peace deep within you.

4. As you continue on this walking path, start to sense the quiet and peaceful sound of water moving over rocks. The sound of water starts to become louder as you come across a waterfall. See a rainbow of light shining through the droplets of water in this waterfall. The waterfall empties into a pool of water. There is a big flat rock in this pool.

5. Step onto the flat rock and sit down. As your breath becomes even more relaxed, imagine that you are part of this rock. As you sit quietly on this rock, notice the leaves and twigs floating by. These leaves and twigs represent the things going on in your life, your concerns. Watch as these concerns float away.

6. Notice how your body and mind are feeling at this time. As you continue to sit quietly, think of goals and dreams you might have in your heart. Using your

@ WEB LINKS

Natural Surroundings

Positive Outlooks. This Facebook page contains great quotes and images from nature. www.facebook.com/positiveoutlooks?sk=wall#!/positiveoutlooks

Labyrinths

- World-Wide Labyrinth Locator. Use this site to find labyrinths around the world. http://labyrinthlocator.com
- The Labyrinth Society. This organization supports people who create, maintain, and use labyrinths. http://labyrinthsociety.org
- Labyrinth Information. www.lessons4living.com/labyrinth.htm

courage and inner strengths, imagine yourself accomplishing these heartfelt goals and dreams.

7. Taking some energizing breaths, stand up, step off the rock, and head back along the walking path, back to your car and home.

FINISH

Take a moment to affirm a positive outlook for your day and appreciate your ability to use your creativity and imagination to relax and focus on your heart's true goals and dreams.

NATURE'S COLORS

This activity includes the peaceful images of nature along with color to help you relax. This activity can be modified for different seasons, such as walking in spring rain and seeing beautiful spring flowers or walking in the winter surrounded by snowflakes.

START

Relaxation pose

CUES

1. Imagine you are walking down a nature trail on a crisp, cool, sunny autumn day. The leaves offer a brilliant fireworks display of yellow, orange, and red. You come to an open area with colorful deciduous trees all around. Sit down comfortably in the middle of all the beautiful colors, textures, and shapes. Imagine you are one of the leaves on the tree. Color your whole body with yellow. As the yellow leaf, drop and flutter slowly to the ground and rest comfortably in a big pile of other colorful leaves.

2. Take a deep, relaxing breath. Imagine you are a leaf on a tree and color your whole body with red. As the red leaf, float slowly to the ground and rest comfortably in a big pile of other leaves.

3. Take a deep, relaxing breath. Imagine you are a leaf on a tree and color your whole body orange. As the orange leaf, glide leisurely to the ground and rest comfortably in a big pile of leaves. Take a deep, relaxing breath and enjoy and be grateful for the beauty of nature.

FINISH

Take a few deep, relaxing breaths while keeping your whole body still and quiet.

ENVIRONMENT MAKEOVER

Environmental Activity

After reviewing the various areas of your environment that may cause stress reactivity (e.g., temperature, air quality, light, color, sound, clutter), choose a personal space to focus on in this activity.

START

Use a journal.

CUES

1. Consider all the areas of the personal space you have chosen. Reflect on how the space is influenced by color, smells, light, technology, clutter, sound, ergonomics, air quality, and temperature.

2. How might you change these aspects of the environment (e.g., better lighting, putting the laptop in another room, buying some candles, painting the room a soothing color, organizing papers into files, getting a fan). Decide what you can change to make your environment less stressful and more conducive to what it is used for, such as sleeping or studying.

FINISH

Reflect on the changes you have made. Many students find that a few small changes can make a big difference in their environments.

Summary

Sometimes we become so accustomed, or numb, to environmental stressors that we do not consider their impact on our wellness. In this chapter we stepped back and took an honest look at how technology, light, temperature, air quality, color, ergonomics, sound, and natural surrounding can cause stress and affect our health.

We also need to consider how our own choices affect the environment and, subsequently, the stress and health of others (e.g., taking our cars for short multiple errands rather than doing several errands at once or carpooling or even walking). One way to contribute to a healthy environment is to reduce, reuse, and recycle. Consider how you contribute to the "unwellness" of the planet and how you might be more green and sustainable in your purchases (e.g., buying products with less packaging, reusing plastic bags, or recycling batteries). Donate items you no longer use rather than dumping them in the trash. Many local charities will appreciate your donations. Advocate for your campus to recycle, and set an example to use these recycling efforts. Another aspect of environmental wellness is consideration of the health and happiness of others—is there an environment of inclusion, respect,

@ WEB LINKS

Peaceful Environments

- M.K. Gandhi Institute for Nonviolence. The mission of this organization is to "help individuals and communities develop the inner resources and practical skill needed to achieve a nonviolent, sustainable and just world." www.gandhiinstitute.org

- Natural Resources Defense Council. The NRDC is considered the United States' foremost environmental action group. www.nrdc.org/about

- The Office of Minority Health. This U.S. government agency is concerned with the health issues of minority groups. Some aspects of the environment, such as pollution in urban areas, adversely affects specific minorities (e.g., asthma in African Americans). http://minorityhealth.hhs.gov

and safety for all? Take a stand if this is not the case by voting, signing petitions, or starting an awareness campaign.

Think about how your own community advocates for the health of its residents. Be aware of health disparities—that is, members of the community who are not getting equal access or opportunities for health information and services.

Throughout this text, we have looked extensively at all dimensions of wellness—physical, emotional, intellectual, social, and spiritual. All of these dimensions play out in our environments, and stress management is difficult when the environment is not conducive to using stress management tools or is itself a stressor (e.g., we can't exercise outdoors because of heat or high pollution levels, or we can't sleep because of urban noise). What steps are you willing to take to change your environment so you are the healthiest and happiest you can be?

epilogue

Congratulations on taking the time to read about stress and stress management. This book offers a considerable amount of evidence to support the importance of practicing stress management in all dimensions of your life to live in balance: physically, emotionally, intellectually, socially, spiritually, and environmentally. I hope you will continue to learn about stress and stress management as they influence the dimensions of your life, and that you will undertake a lifelong journey of practicing stress management. The word *practice* is essential because the consistent repetition of these tools can truly change and transform your life. I hope the tools have been presented in a way that is simple and easy to understand. However, you must make the commitment to practice them on a consistent basis—not just once in a while when stress becomes overwhelming and out of control. The anxiety journal found in the appendix can help act as a reminder for the different stress-management tools discussed throughout the book that you should consider when you are dealing with stress and anxiety. Making stress management a lifelong goal is all of our responsibility. When we practice self-care, others can be inspired to do so as well. Be ready to be part of a critical mass of people who realize the importance of stress management to their health and happiness.

Be well.
Nanette Tummers

ANXIETY JOURNAL

Using a journal to process anxious moments can help you pinpoint sources of anxiety and find tools to use to cope with them.

START

Find a quiet place. Take a few deep, centering breaths. Take a few minutes to reflect on how anxiety, fear, and worry play a role in your life right now and assess your reactivity to stressful events. Consider how these negative events affect your total health.

CUES

1. In the first row of the journal table, describe the situation that is causing anxiety.

2. Within each subsequent row, jot down ways these events affect you holistically and how you could use various emotion-based stress management tools to deal with the situation.

Anxiety Journal

In the first row of the journal table, describe the situation that is causing anxiety. In each subsequent row, jot down ways you could use the various stress management tools.

Anxiety-causing situation	
Thought stopping	
Reframing	
Positive self-talk	
Breath strategy	
Social support	
Environmental management	
Relaxation strategy	

From N. Tummers, 2013, *Stress Management: A Wellness Approach* (Champaign, IL: Human Kinetics).

The Anxiety Journal can be found in the appendix.

FINISH

What specific actions could you take to accept and deal positively with these difficult events? Keep in mind the concept of an internal locus of control.

Set an intention with an action step to use one or more of the stress management tools when you are feeling anxious physically, emotionally or intellectually. *I will* _____.

appendix

Worksheets

A Journey Begins With a Single Step

Your journey of learning more about stress and stress management begins with paying attention to how stressful events manifest in you—in your body, emotions, and thoughts.

Stressful event	How does it feel in my body?	How do I feel emotionally?	What thoughts are associated with this event?

From N. Tummers, 2013, *Stress Management: A Wellness Approach* (Champaign, IL: Human Kinetics).

Physical Activity Log

Date	Physical activity (What did you do?)	Intensity level: mild (0-4); moderate (5-7); high (8-10)	Length (minutes)	Enjoyment level (0 = none; 10 = a lot)	Support	Barriers

From N. Tummers, 2013, *Stress Management: A Wellness Approach* (Champaign, IL: Human Kinetics).

Sleep Log

Date	Sleep time	Quality of your sleep: low (0-3); adequate (4-7); refreshed (8-10)	Sleep routine (e.g., took a warm shower; shut off electronics)	How quickly you fell asleep and whether you stayed sleep (e.g., was interrupted by text at 3 a.m.)	Activity four hours prior to sleep time (e.g., physical activity; argument)	Any other observations

From N. Tummers, 2013, *Stress Management: A Wellness Approach* (Champaign, IL: Human Kinetics).

Journaling About Assertiveness in My Life

	Giving	Receiving
Criticism		
Acknowledging needs and rights		
Expressing negative feelings		
Expressing positive feelings		
Acknowledging compliments		
Accepting differing opinions		
Making requests		
Being fully present and not distracted		
Saying no		
Listening without interrupting		

From N. Tummers, 2013, *Stress Management: A Wellness Approach* (Champaign, IL: Human Kinetics).

Anxiety Journal

In the first row of the journal table, describe the situation that is causing anxiety. In each subsequent row, jot down ways you could use the various stress management tools.

Anxiety-causing situation	
Thought stopping	
Reframing	
Positive self-talk	
Breath strategy	
Social support	
Environmental management	
Relaxation strategy	

From N. Tummers, 2013, *Stress Management: A Wellness Approach* (Champaign, IL: Human Kinetics).

references and resources

Adams, K., Kohlmeier, M., & Zeisel, S. (2010). Nutrition education in U.S. medical schools: Latest update of a national survey. *Academic Medicine* 85 (9): 1537-1542.

Amen, D. (2008). *Magnificent mind at any age*. New York: Three Rivers Press.

American College Health Association. (2011). National College Health Assessment: Report Spring 2011. www.acha-ncha.org/reports_ACHA-NCHAII.html

American Massage Therapy Association. (n.d.). Position statement proposal on public health initiatives. www.amtamassage.org/uploads/cms/documents/ps12-02_massage_and_public_health.pdf

American Psychological Association. (2012). Stress in America: Our health at risk. www.apa.org/news/press/releases/stress/index.aspx

American Psychological Association. (n.d.a). Depression. www.apa.org/topics/depress/index.aspx

American Psychological Association. (n.d.b). Psychological topics: Anger. www.apa.org/topics/anger/index.aspx

Anderson, C. (2001) Heat and violence. *Current Directions in Psychological Science* 10 (1): 33-38.

Astin, A., Astin, H., & Lindholm, J. (2004). A national study of spirituality in higher education: Students' search for meaning and purpose: Key findings of the first national longitudinal study of undergraduates' spiritual growth. Los Angeles: Higher Education Research Institute Graduate School of Education & Information Studies, University of California at Los Angeles. http://spirituality.ucla.edu/findings/

Azeemi, S., & Raza, M. (2005). A critical analysis of chromotherapy and its scientific evolution. *Evidence Based Complementary and Alternative Medicine* 2 (4): 481-488.

Bandura, A. (1986). *Social foundation of thought and action*. Englewood Cliffs, NJ: Prentice Hall.

Barnes, P.M., Bloom, B., & Nahin, R. (2008). Complementary and alternative medicine use among adults and children: United States, 2007. *National health statistics reports, no. 12*. Hyattsville, MD: National Center for Health Statistics.

Benson, H. (1975, 2000). *The relaxation response*. New York: HarperCollins.

Beresin, E. (2010). The impact of media violence on children and adolescents: Opportunities for clinical interventions. American Academy of Child and Adolescent Psychiatry. www.aacap.org/cs/root/developmentor/the_impact_of_media_violence_on_children_and_adolescents_opportunities_for_clinical_interventions

Berkman, L., & Sym, S. (1979). Social networks, host resistance, and mortality: A nine-year follow-up of Alameda County residents. *American Journal of Epidemiology* 109: 186-204.

Bosma-den Boer, B., van Welten, M., & Priumboom, L. (2012). Chronic inflammatory diseases are stimulated by current lifestyle: How diet, stress levels and medication prevent our bodies from recovering. *Nutrition & Metabolism* 9: 32.

Burns, D. (1999). *The feeling good handbook*. New York: Plume.

Byrd, R. (1988). Positive therapeutic effects of intercessory prayer in a coronary care unit population. *Southern Medical Journal* 81 (7): 826-829.

Carver, C.S. (2006). Sources of Social Support Scale. University of Miami, Department of Psychology. www.psy.miami.edu/faculty/ccarver/sclSSSS.html

Childre, D., Martin, H., & Beech, D. (2000). *The HeartMath solution: The Institute of HeartMath's revolutionary program for engaging the power of the heart's intelligence.* New York: Harper-Collins.

Childs, E., O'Connor, S., & de Wit, H. (2011). Bidirectional interactions between acute psychosocial stress and acute intravenous alcohol in healthy men. *Alcoholism: Clinical and Experimental Research* 35: 1794-1803.

Connor, D. (2005). *Undoing perpetual stress.* New York: Berkley Trade/Penguin Books.

Core Institute. (2011, November 1). Core alcohol and drug survey. Executive summary. http://core.siu.edu/pdfs/report09.pdf

Cornell, J. (2006). *Mandala: Luminous symbols for healing.* Wheaton, IL: Quest Books.

Cousins, N. (1979). *Anatomy of an illness as perceived by the patient.* New York: W.W. Norton & Company.

Csikszentmihalyi, M. (1997). *Finding flow: The psychology of engagement with everyday life.* New York: Basic Books.

Dartmouth University Academic Skills Center. (2012). Improving concentration, memory, and motivation. www.dartmouth.edu/~acskills/success/study.html

Davidson, R., Kabat-Zinn, J., Schumacher, J., Rosenkranz, M., Muller, D., Santorelli, S. Urbanowski, F., Harrington, A., Bonus, K., & Sheridan, J. (2003). Alterations in brain and immune function produced by mindfulness meditation. *Psychosomatic Medicine* 65: 564-570.

Dossey, L. (1995). *Healing words: The power of prayer and the practice of medicine.* New York: HarperOne.

Dyer, W. (1976). *Your erroneous zones.* New York: Avon Books.

Eliot, L. (2009, September 8). Girl brain, boy brain? *Scientific American.* www.scientificamerican.com/article.cfm?id=girl-brain-boy-brain

Ellis, A. (2001). *Overcoming destructive beliefs, feelings, and behaviors.* Amherst, NY: Prometheus Books.

Emmons, R. (2011). The Gratitude Questionnaire (GQ-6) document. http://psychology.ucdavis.edu/Labs/emmons/PWT/index.cfm?Section=5

Emmons, R.A., & McCullough, M.E. (2003). Counting blessings versus burdens: Experimental studies of gratitude and subjective well-being in daily life. *Journal of Personality and Social Psychology* 84: 377-389.

Fine, A. (Ed.). (2010). *Handbook on animal-assisted therapy: Theoretical foundations and guidelines for practice* (3rd ed.). Boston: Academic Press.

Finkelstein, J. (2006). Maslow's hierarchy of needs. http://en.wikipedia.org/wiki/Image:Maslow%27s_hierarchy_of_needs.png

Fontana, D. (2005). *Meditating with mandalas.* London: Duncan Baird.

Fredrickson, B. (2009). *Positivity: Groundbreaking research reveals how to embrace the hidden strength of positive emotions, overcome negativity and thrive.* New York: Crown.

Gardner, H. (1983). *Frames of mind: The theory of multiple intelligences.* New York: Basic Books.

George, L., Larsons, D., Koeing, H., & McCullough, M. (2009). Spirituality and health: What we know, what we need to know. *Journal of Social and Clinical Psychology* 19 (1): 102-116.

Gershon, M. (1998). *The second brain.* New York: HarperCollins.

Gilmour, J., & Williams, L. (2012). Type D personality is associated with maladaptive health-related behaviours. *Journal of Health Psychology* 17 (4): 471-478.

Gladwell, M. (2008). *Outliers: The story of success.* New York: Little, Brown.

Goleman, D. (2000). *Working with emotional intelligence.* New York: Bantam Books.

Goleman, D. (2011). New insights on emotional intelligence. [Podcast]. http://podcast.mwm-claughlin.com/podcasts/daniel-goleman

Grassi, A., Gaggioli, A., & Riva, G. (2009). The green valley: The use of mobile narratives for reducing stress in commuters. *CyberPsychology & Behavior* 12 (2): 155-161.

Greenberg, J. (2008). *Comprehensive stress management* (10th ed.). Boston: McGraw-Hill Higher Ed.

Harvard University Newsletter. (2012, May). Blue light has a dark side. www.health.harvard.edu/newsletters/Harvard_Health_Letter/2012/May/blue-light-has-a-dark-side

Hawks, S., Hull, M., Thalman, R., & Richins, P. (1995). Review of spiritual health: Definition, role, and intervention strategies in health promotion. *American Journal of Health Promotion* 9 (5): 371-378.

Heschong Mahone Group. (1999). Daylighting in schools. http://centerforgreenschools.org/docs/heschong-mahone-daylighting-study.pdf

Hölzel, B.K., Carmody, J., Vangel, M., Congleton, C., Yerramsetti, S.M., Gard, T., & Lazar, S.W. (2011). Mindfulness practice leads to increases in regional brain gray matter density. *Psychiatry Research: Neuroimaging* 191 (1): 36-43.

Institute of Medicine Panel on Dietary Reference Intakes for Electrolytes and Water, Standing Committee on the Scientific Evaluation of Dietary Reference Intakes. (2005). *Dietary reference intakes for water, potassium, sodium, chloride, and sulfate.* Washington, DC: The National Academies Press.

International Forgiveness Institute. (n.d.). Summary of Dr. Enright research. www.internationalforgiveness.com/data/uploaded/files/ExamplesOfExperimentalStudies.pdf

Jacobsen, E. (1978). *You must relax: Practical methods for reducing the tensions of modern living* (5th ed.). New York: McGraw-Hill.

Jahnke, R., Larkey, L., Rogers, C., Etnier, J., & Lin, F. (2010). A comprehensive review of health benefits of qigong and tai chi. *American Journal of Health Promotion* 24 (6): e1-e25.

Jobs, S. (2009, September 19). Steve Jobs explains the rules of success. www.youtube.com/watch?v=KuNQgln6TL0&feature=related

Kabat-Zinn, J. (2009, July 31-August 2). Proceedings of the Mindfulness and Education Retreat: Bringing mindfulness practice to children grades K-12. Rhinebeck, NY: Omega Institute.

Karren, K., Smith, N., Hafen, B., & Jenkins, K. (2010). *Mind/body health: The effects of attitudes, emotions, and relationships* (4th ed.). San Francisco: Pearson Benjamin Cummings.

Katz, D., Doughty, K., & Ali, A. (2011). Cocoa and chocolate in human health and disease. *Antioxidants & Redox Signaling* 15 (10): 2779-2781. www.ncbi.nlm.nih.gov/pubmed/21470061

Kobasa, S.C. (1979). Stressful life events, personality and health: An inquiry into hardiness. *Journal of Personality and Social Psychology* 37: 1-11.

Kocalevent, R., Levenstein, S., Fliege, H., Schmid, G., Hinz, A., Brähler, E., & Klapp, B.F. (2007). Contribution to the construct validity of the Perceived Stress Questionnaire from a population-based survey. *Journal of Psychosomatic Research* 63 (1): 71-81.

Kohls, K., Sauer, S., Offenbächer, M., & Giordano, J. (2011). Spirituality: An overlooked predictor of placebo effects? *Philosophical Transactions of the Royal Society B: Biological Sciences* 366 (1572): 1838-1848. doi: 10.1098/rstb.2010.0389

Kornfield, J. (2008). *Meditation for beginners.* Boulder, CO: Sounds True.

Lane, J. (2011). Caffeine, glucose metabolism, and type-2 diabetes. *Journal of Caffeine Research* 1 (1): 23-28.

Lane, J., Pieper, C., Phllips-Bute, B., Bryant, J., & Kuhn, C. (2002). Caffeine affects cardiovascular and neuroendocrine activation at work and home. *Psychosomatic Medicine* 64: 595-603.

Lazar, S., Kerr, C., Wasserman, R., Gray, J., Greve, D., Treadway, M., McGarvey, M., Quinn, B., Dusek, J., Benson, H., Rauch, S., Moore, C., & Fischl, B. (2005). Meditation experience is associated with increased cortical thickness. *Neuroreport* 16 (17): 1893-1897.

Linde, K., Allais, G., Brinkhaus, B., Manheimer, E., Vickers, A., & White, A.R. (2009). Acupuncture for tension-type headache. *Cochrane Database of Systematic Reviews* (1): CD00758.

Luks, A. (1988). Helper's high: Volunteering makes people feel good, physically and emotionally. *Psychology Today* 22 (10): 34-42.

Luskin, F. (2003). *Forgive for good.* New York: HarperOne.

Luskin, F.M., Ginzburg, K., & Thoresen, C.E. (2005). The effect of forgiveness training on psychosocial factors in college age adults. *Humboldt Journal of Social Relations. Special Issue: Altruism, Intergroup Apology and Forgiveness: Antidote for a Divided World* 29 (2): 163-184.

Lutz, A., Brefczynski-Lewis, J., Johnstone, T., & Davidson, R.J. (2008). Regulation of the neural circuitry of emotion by compassion meditation: Effects of meditative expertise. *PLoS ONE* 3 (3): e1897.

Lyubomirsky, S. (2007). *The how of happiness: A scientific approach to getting the life you want.* New York: Penguin Press.

Lyubomirsky, S., King, L., & Diener, E. (2005). The benefits of frequent positive affect: Does happiness lead to success? *Psychological Bulletin* 131 (6): 803-855.

Maslow, A. (1997). *Motivation and personality* (3rd ed.). New York: HarperCollins College.

Maslow, A. (2011). *Toward a psychology of being* (3rd ed.). Radford, VA: Wilder.

Matud, M.P. (2004). Gender differences in stress and coping styles. *Personality and Individual Differences* 37 (7): 1401-1415.

McEwen, B. (2005). Stressed or stressed out: What is the difference? *Journal of Psychiatry & Neuroscience* 30 (5): 315.

McEwen, B., & Lasley, E. (2002). *The end of stress as we know it.* Washington, DC: National Academies Press.

Medical Dictionary. (n.d.a). Caffeine. http://medical-dictionary.thefreedictionary.com/caffeine

Medical Dictionary. (n.d.b). White refined sugar. http://medical-dictionary.thefreedictionary.com/White+refined+sugar

Miller, M. (2005, November). What is type D personality? *Harvard Medical Health Letter.* 8.

Morris, T., Moore, M., & Morris, F. (2011). Stress and chronic illness: The case of diabetes. *Journal of Adult Development* 18: 70-80.

Nahin, R.L., Barnes, P.M., Stussman, B.J., & Bloom, B. (2009). Costs of complementary and alternative medicine (CAM) and frequency of visits to CAM practitioners: United States, 2007. *National health statistics reports, no. 18.* Hyattsville, MD: National Center for Health Statistics.

National Center for Complementary and Alternative Medicine. (2007). *The use of complementary and alternative medicine in the United States.* http://nccam.nih.gov/news/camstats/2007/camsurvey_fs1.htm

National Center for Complementary and Alternative Medicine. (2009). Ayurvedic medicine: An introduction. National Institute of Health. http://nccam.nih.gov/health/ayurveda/introduction.htm

National Center for Complementary and Alternative Medicine. (2011). *Downloadable graphics on CAM costs in the United States.* http://nccam.nih.gov/news/camstats/costs/graphics.htm

National Institute of General Medical Sciences. (n.d.). Circadian rhythms fact sheet. National Institute of Health. www.nigms.nih.gov/Education/Factsheet_CircadianRhythms.htm

National Institute of Neurological Disorders and Stroke. (2012). Headache: Hope through research. www.ninds.nih.gov/disorders/headache/detail_headache.htm

National Sleep Foundation. (2011). Sleep in America poll: 2011 report: Communications technology and sleep. Washington, DC: The Foundation.

National Sleep Foundation. (n.d.). Sleep topics. www.sleepfoundation.org/articles/sleep-topics?page=1

Nichter, M., Nichter, M., & Carkoglu, A. (2007). Reconsidering stress and smoking: A qualitative study among college students. *Tobacco Control* 16: 211-214.

Nidich, S.I., Rainforth, M.V., Haaga, D.A.F., et al. (2009, December). A randomized controlled trial on the effects of the Transcendental Meditation program on blood pressure, psychological distress, and coping in young adults. *American Journal of Hypertension* 22 (12): 1326-1333.

O'Connor, R. (2005). *Undoing perpetual stress. The missing connection between depression, anxiety and 21st century illness.* New York: Berkley Books, pp. 195-199.

Pelletier, K., & Herzing, D. (1988). Psychoneuroimmunology: Toward a mind-body model. *Advances* 5 (1): 27-56.

Pet Partners. (n.d.). Animal-assisted activities. www.petpartners.org/page.aspx?pid=319

Pink, D. (2011). *Drive: The surprising truth about what motivates us.* New York: Riverhead Books.

Reivich, K., & Shatte, A. (2002). *The resilience factor: 7 keys to finding inner strength and overcoming life's hurdles.* New York: Broadway Books.

Rose Park Labyrinth Medical Center of Central Georgia. (n.d.). 3 minutes chakra test. www.lessons4living.com/rose_park.htm

Rossman, M. (2010). *The worry solution.* New York: Crown Archetype.

Rubin, G. (2009). *The happiness project.* New York: HarperCollins.

Salmon, P. (2001). Effects of physical exercise on anxiety, depression, and sensitivity to stress: A unifying theory. *Clinical Psychology Review* 21 (1): 33-61.

Saltzman, A. (n.d.). Mindfulness-based stress reduction for school-age children. www.stillquietplace.com/wp-content/uploads/2010/11/Saltzman-Grecco2.pdf

Sapolsky, R. (2004). *Why zebras don't get ulcers.* New York: Holt Paperbacks.

Seligman, M. (2011). *Flourish: A visionary new understanding of happiness and well-being.* New York: Free Press.

Seligman, M., Reivich, K., Jaycox, L., & Gillham, J. (2007). *The optimistic child: A proven program to safeguard children against depression and build lifelong resilience.* New York: Houghton Mifflin.

Selye, H. (1970). The evolution of the stress concept: Stress and cardiovascular disease. *The American Journal of Cardiology* 26 (3): 289-299.

Sime, W. (2007). Exercise therapy as stress management. In Lehrer, P., Woolfolk, R., & Sime, W. (Eds.), *Principles and practice of stress management* (3rd ed., pp. 333-359). New York: The Guilford Press.

Snodgrass, S. (1986, August 22-26). *The effects of walking behavior on mood.* Paper presented at the Annual Convention of the American Psychological Association, Washington, DC.

Southwick, S., Vythilingam, M., & Charney, D. (2005). The psychobiology of depression and resilience to stress: Implications for prevention and treatment. *Annual Review of Clinical Psychology* 1: 255-291.

Tao Te Ching. (n.d.). The tao of stress. www.centertao.org/forum/discussion/569/the-tao-of-stress/

Taylor, S., Klein, L., Lewis, B., Gruenewald, T., Gurung, R., & Updegraff, J. (2000). Bio behavioral response to stress in females: Tend-and-befriend, not flight-or-flight. *Psychological Review* 107: 411-429.

Thich Nhat Hahn. (1999). *The miracle of mindfulness. An introduction to the practice of meditation.* Boston: Beacon Press.

Tiffany, S., Agnew, C., Maylath, N., Dierker, L., Flaherty, B., Richardson, E., Balster, R., Segress, M., Clayton, R., & the Tobacco Etiology Research Network (TERN). (2007). Smoking in college freshmen: University project of the Tobacco Etiology Research Network (UpTERN). *Nicotine & Tobacco Research* 9 (Suppl 4): S611-S625.

Touch Research Institute. (n.d.). Research at TRI. Touch Research Institute, University of Miami, Miller School of Medicine, Miami, Florida. www6.miami.edu/touch-research/Research.html

University of Maryland Medical Center. (2011). Aromatherapy. www.umm.edu/altmed/articles/aromatherapy-000347.htm

U.S. Centers for Disease Control and Prevention. (2011a). Alcohol use and health. www.cdc.gov/alcohol/fact-sheets/alcohol-use.htm

U.S. Centers for Disease Control and Prevention. (2011b). Nutrition for everyone: Protein. www.cdc.gov/nutrition/everyone/basics/protein.html#How much protein

U.S. Centers for Disease Control and Prevention. (2012). Binge drinking: Nationwide problem, local solutions. www.cdc.gov/vitalsigns/BingeDrinking/index.html

U.S. Department of Agriculture. (n.d.). Protein foods gallery. www.choosemyplate.gov/food-groups/food_library/proteinfoods/almonds.html

U.S. Department of Labor, Office of Safety and Health Administration. (n.d.). Ergonomics. www.osha.gov/SLTC/ergonomics

U.S. Environmental Protection Agency. (2009). Air quality index: A guide to air quality and your health. www.epa.gov/airnow/aqi_brochure_08-09.pdf

U.S. Environmental Protective Agency. (n.d.). Noise pollution. www.epa.gov/air/noise.html

U.S. Navy. (n.d.). Fitness, sports and deployed forces support: Hydrate. www.navyfitness.org/nutrition/noffs_fueling_series/hydrate

Wardle, J., Chida, Y., Gibson, E.L., Whitaker, K.L., & Steptoe, A. (2011). Stress and adiposity: A meta-analysis of longitudinal studies. *Obesity* 19: 771-778.

Winner, J. (2008). *Take the stress out of your life*. Philadelphia: Da Capo Press, p. 24.

World Health Organization. (2012). Health topics: Depression. www.who.int/topics/depression/en

World Health Organization. (n.d.). Global Health Observatory: Risk factors. www.who.int/gho/ncd/risk_factors/en/index.html

Yale School of Medicine. (n.d.). Winter depression research clinic. http://psychiatry.yale.edu/research/programs/clinical_people/winter.aspx

Yamada, K. (2009). *How many people does it take to make a difference?* Seattle: Compendium.

Yerkes, R.M., & Dodson, J.D. (1908). The relation of strength of stimulus to rapidity of habit-formation. *Journal of Comparative Neurology and Psychology* 18: 459-482.

Yusuf, S., Hawken, S., Ounpuu, S., Dans, T., Avezum, A., et al. (2004). Effect of potentially modifiable risk factors associated with myocardial infarction in 52 countries (the INTERHEART study): Case-control study. *Lancet* 364: 937-952.

index

about the author

Nanette E. Tummers, EdD, is a professor of health and physical education at Eastern Connecticut State University. A certified holistic stress management instructor, Tummers has developed and taught traditional and online stress management courses at the university level since 2005. She has taught stress management courses to other populations as well, including high-risk populations, cancer patients, and athletes.

Tummers also trains educators in providing stress management activities for K-12 students, and she has developed ancillaries for stress management texts. She remains active in conducting research in positive psychology, peer mentoring, and stress management and has presented on these topics at the national AAHPERD conference. Tummers is the author of two additional books published by Human Kinetics, Teaching Yoga for Life (2009) and Teaching Stress Management (2011).

In her leisure time, she enjoys hiking and volunteering.